Conflict and Communication

CONFLICT &

COMMUNICATION

The Use of

Controlled Communication

in International Relations

JOHN W. BURTON

Reader in International Relations, and
Director of the Centre for the Analysis of Conflict,
University College London

 The Free Press, New York

UNIVERSITY COLLEGE LONDON

Centre for the Analysis of Conflict

In 1966, University College London established a Centre for the Analysis of Conflict for the purpose of studying communal and international conflict. A major research activity of the Centre has consisted of private discussions between parties to current international disputes or to disputes between communities within states. Present have been political and social scientists who controlled and took an active part in discussions. These meetings helped in the formulation of hypotheses and led to theoretical and empirical studies.

University College has received support from the Joseph Rowntree Charitable Trust, the Social Science Research Council of the United Kingdom and the Carnegie Endowment for International Peace. At an earlier stage, and before support could be sought, a pilot study was made possible by the generous hospitality of the Ciba Foundation, London.

The views expressed in this and other publications of the Centre are those of the authors.

G. W. KEETON
Chairman of the Board of Management
of the Centre for the Analysis of Conflict

Contents

Introduction

This is a report on the use of a technique by which political and social scientists exercised control of discussions between representatives of nations and states that were involved in conflict. The name 'controlled communication' is employed as this seems best to describe what in practice took place. The technique has some features in common with 'casework', the method used by social workers in the handling of individuals who are in conflict with their social environment. It has some features in common with procedures of conciliation and mediation increasingly employed in the handling of industrial and small group conflicts. All have in common the absence of enforcement and the encouragement of self-adjusting processes; but 'controlled communication' is intended to describe a technique that has some special features particularly suited to the nature of international and inter-state conflict.

The distinctive hypothesis is that the conflict behaviour of communities and states comprises alterable components such as perception of external conditions, selection of goals from many possible values, choice of different means of attaining goals, and assessments of values and means in relation to assessments of costs of conflict. The method hypothesises that conflicts of interests are subjective, and that experience and knowledge alter these components, thus producing altered relationships. By controlled communication misperceptions that parties to a dispute have of each other are exposed by introducing relevant theoretical and empirical knowledge, and a condition is created in which considered hypotheses and propositions compensate in some degree for the uncertainties of the behaviour of others, and of forecasting. While no bargaining or negotiation takes place, preconditions of agreement may be established.

The method has been used with two different objectives. Originally it was employed as a means by which an analysis could be made of inter-nation and inter-state conflicts. The research programme of the Centre for the Analysis of Conflict arose out of a belief that official, historical, journalistic, and even analytically descriptive accounts written up after a crisis, cannot provide answers to many of the questions that are prompted by contemporary interdisciplinary studies of world politics. These can be answered only by analysing perceptions and misperceptions, interactions and features of state decision-making, which are best observed when the parties in conflict are in an interacting situation. The obviously desirable procedure was to select a current conflict, preferably one in which there was actual violence, and to create a situation in which the parties involved would expose their perceptions of each other, their motivations and goals, their internal political problems, their interpretations of events that led to the conflict and then to its escalation, and anything else to which contemporary theories of relations between states and of conflict might point. Accordingly, in 1965 a request was made to the governments directly involved in a particularly interesting conflict, to cooperate in this academic enquiry by sending representatives who could reflect the views of their governments, to take part in discussions in the presence of a panel of political and social scientists. It was made clear that the exercise was an academic one, and that the purpose was not conciliation or mediation, and not to settle the conflict – though it was hoped that the communication established between the parties would be helpful to them. There was a cooperative and generous response, and discussions took place in London, where they continued for one week, and meetings were held from time to time subsequently.

This was an academic exercise that had a particular and limited research purpose. However, it was clear that it was most rewarding academically, and if repeated in relation to other types of conflict could lead to insights and hypotheses, and perhaps to means of testing propositions. Furthermore, the experience suggested that an important technique might have been evolved, as it were by accident, for the avoidance of conflict, and for the resolution of conflict even during violence, because the parties themselves seemed to gain from the exercise in some ways not possible from more traditional procedures of conciliation, arbitration and negotiation. Thus the method came to have a second objective – the resolution of conflict. Visits were made to other governments that were involved in conflict situations to see whether they would cooperate in the same manner. More careful consideration was given to the preparation of propositions prior to discussions, to techniques, and to means of recording and processing data generated. In 1966 similar discussions took place between two national groups that were involved in violence, and the technique of controlled communication underwent change and development. In the light of these experiences discussions were held with representatives of other governments involved in conflict, and studies were made of aspects of other situations, of the literature on conflict, and of the history of traditional forms of mediation. It is now appropriate to make a report on the uses of controlled communication, and to examine its potential and limitations, as a means both of analytical study of world society and of conflict resolution and avoidance.

The apparent concentration upon conflict as the phenomenon being studied should not divert attention from the purpose of the study of conflict, which is the gaining of insights into world politics generally. It is clear that breakdowns and inefficiencies in performance attract more of our attention than the smooth working of systems. This is as true of a political or social system as it is of a mechanical one; a case of apparent harmony of social interest does not attract our attention as does one of antagonism. This may explain in part why conflict has been important in social studies – industrial strikes, delinquency and small group conflict. It probably accounts in part for the evident interest of philosophers, historians, lawyers, biologists, political scientists, economists, psychologists, anthropologists and sociologists in international conflict. There is, however, a broader academic interest in conflict. There is an interest in the operation of the system concerned, how it works, why it broke down, how it can be altered to improve its efficiency, and how other systems of a similar construction operate. The study of conflict is not merely because it attracts attention. It is largely because by examining it the normal operation of the system can better be understood.

In practice, analysis and resolution of conflict cannot readily be conducted separately. The means of resolution are to some extent suggested by an analysis of the nature of the conflict being examined, and of conflict generally. Resolution itself tends to emerge out of accurate analysis. At the same time analysis is promoted by the experience of attempting resolution. In any area of science scientific advance is promoted by application. Mechanical engineers, and some medical and social workers, have an immediate responsibility for and interest in repairing breakdowns. This greatly stimulates research into the general operations of the system concerned. Practice and research in these cases are one and the same operation. Knowledge advances rapidly when the practitioner is research-minded, and when the research worker is operationally-minded. There has not been this interplay between operation and research in the field of international politics. The academic interest in international conflict has been almost confined to the broader one; conflicts have been studied, not to stop particular ones, but as a means of understanding the international political system, both its peaceful and its violent aspects. Indeed, scholars have tended to avoid the responsibilities of the practitioner: they have hesitated to examine contemporary breakdowns in social organisations, such as are evidenced by wars, preferring to make their analysis only much later when documents are available. The purpose of controlled communication is to provide a clinical framework, and a means by which an applied science of International Relations can develop.

This is not to say that analysis of conflict is sufficient for purposes of explaining behaviour. On the contrary, one of the major reasons why the study of international politics was at a virtual standstill before the forties was to a large degree due to the concentration by diplomatic historians on crises, and to the neglect of the basic reciprocal transactions which are as widespread as they are inconspicuous. Theoretical works on integration are of great value in the study of any society. They have been valuable in this research project: both in analysis and resolution of conflict concepts of norm behaviour are necessary, and studies of integration help to provide them.

It can be anticipated that this study of controlled communication will rest a great deal upon knowledge of relationships and response of behavioural units other than nations and states. Not only is the method of face-to-face communication drawn from other disciplines, but the features of relationships upon which it focuses attention – perception, responses, feed-back, decision-making – have been examined in other contexts. International politics is an interdisciplinary study, and this technique is one means of taking advantage of empirical work in other disciplines. This is not an unexpected step in the study of world society. These are means of analysis and scientific method common to all behavioural sciences. Furthermore, General Systems Theory is more and more integrating the study of international politics with the study of politics generally, and the study of world society with the study of any society and with separate aspects of it. While there are few direct applications of the findings of any one discipline to another, while the behaviour of states cannot necessarily be deduced from findings about the behaviour of individuals and small groups, some deductive reasoning is possible within a systems framework. If, for example, it is being found in social life that coercion is a less effective means of bringing about a degree of social conformity than is the integration of the individual with his environment, then there is reason for believing that this might be the case also in relation to larger systems and their environments. Furthermore, the methods by which changes are brought about in one system are likely to be capable of adaptation to others.

The conclusions of this study are critical of traditional methods of mediation, conciliation and arbitration on the

grounds that these, like the more formal judicial procedures from which they derive, are not wholly relevant to
the nature of world society. Behavioural experience and
traditional approaches to conflict are brought into sharp
relief. Empirical studies offer little support for traditional
beliefs in world order through world law, for the view that
states should be obliged to submit to third party decisions,
or for the claim that international institutions require
powers of enforcement. Resolution of conflict is a process
that comes from the decision-making of the parties. It
involves a reappraisal of values and alternatives and costs,
and the appropriate international institution is one that
facilitates this process. It is critical also of traditional
diplomatic practices. International studies have tended
to be conducted separately from contemporary diplomatic practice, and, on the other hand, the practice of
diplomacy has been little influenced by research. No such
watertight compartments are now possible. Diplomacy is
becoming as much exposed to scientific scrutiny as is any
branch of social policy, despite traditions of secrecy that
are maintained. In conditions of controlled communication, in which scholars have opportunities to pose questions that seem significant to them on the basis of their
theories, in which parties are endeavouring to explain
their behaviour, relevant influences are revealed. Academic criticism is, however, designed to be constructive,
and the hope is that this report will stimulate a dialogue
with lawyers and diplomats in addition to other scholars
in this field of studies.

The Centre does not confine itself to this face-to-face
analysis; on the contrary, most of the time of its members
is taken up with keeping in touch with developments in
theory, examining similar techniques employed in other
social sciences, making comparative studies and typologies

of conflict, pursuing field studies, and advancing hypotheses in theoretical writings. The conduct of the actual
case studies, and the processing of data generated, rest
upon this theoretical and empirical work. The time
spent on analysis in a controlled face-to-face situation is
an important source of hypotheses. My *Systems, States,
Diplomacy and Rules*, published in 1968, which is a
theoretical analysis, is one direct outcome of these experiences. This and the present study of the technique are
complementary, and the expression 'see companion study'
is used as a convenient form of cross-reference. There are
many cross-references, and some deliberate reiterations;
even so a great deal of the argument that is contained in
the theoretical study is assumed in this.

Part One is concerned with description of the technique
of controlled communication: a report on research done.
In Part Two an assessment is made of its significance.
Because this method has been used both for analysis and
for resolution, it is desirable to trace separately historical
trends in the analysis of international relations and in the
handling of conflict. Controlled communication will be
shown to be a technique both of analysis and of resolution
consistent with these separate trends. In making a brief
historical survey of these trends assumptions are revealed
that have traditionally been held about the behaviour of
states, and attention is thereby directed to other assumptions implicit in controlled communication.

It will be appreciated that the discussions that take
place between nominees of parties to disputes must be in
private. Even the fact that they are taking place cannot be
made known at the time, especially in conditions in which
there are actual hostilities. Consequently, in a published
report it is not possible to refer to the details of discussion.
This does not hinder the writing of this report for it is

concerned with procedures and techniques. Discussions with political leaders outside the controlled framework are also in confidence. This prevents adequate acknowledgement of the ready cooperation of politicians and officials who have given freely of their time, in some cases in order to explain reasons why they could not be involved in a controlled communication, which is of academic interest in a study of method.

I have had the opportunity of discussing the ideas put forward in this book with members of a study group on international organisation convened by the European Centre of the Carnegie Endowment for International Peace at Geneva. These discussions helped to bring to the surface aspects that might not have been dealt with adequately, and my particular thanks are due to the members of that group, to J. Goormaghtigh and J. Siotis of the Geneva office, and to J. Johnson and Anne Winslow in New York, for their cooperation and advice in this and related projects.

Academic colleagues from several countries have contributed to the programme of the Centre. Some have taken part in controlled discussions, and some in seminars that precede and follow them. While it would be unfair to identify any one of them with any particular views expressed here, in fact all made a contribution to them. Special thanks are due to my colleagues in the Centre, M. H. Banks, C. R. Mitchell and M. B. Nicholson, and to R. F. H. Austin, L. Burton, A. V. S. de Reuck, A. J. R. Groom, R. Higgins and A. N. Oppenheim, who discussed this report at various stages of drafting and to A. McClelland who prepared the Index.

PART ONE

CONTROLLED COMMUNICATION

I The Research Setting

The chapters of this first Part deal with the many aspects of controlled communication between parties involved in conflict, for example, problems encountered in determining parties to disputes, means of establishing and controlling communication, and even details such as seating arrangements. As indicated in the Introduction, these are based upon contrived experiences of controlled communication between the representatives of governments in dispute and conflict. However, they have not been written in a descriptive form. Rather the intention is to interpret and possibly to explain what was observed, in retrospect as it were, in the light of theory and the experience of others who have researched in related fields such as industrial conflict. The actual experience of controlled communication served far more the purpose of stimulating hypotheses than of providing evidence of the validity of any proposition. In this sense a description of what took place is not particularly relevant to the observations and propositions that follow. However, a brief description of what took place at the time of discussions will help to provide answers to some questions that will occur to the reader.

In October 1965 invitations, in the form of requests to help in a research project, were sent to three governments. It was stated that an endeavour would be made to define with some precision the persistent features of the relations between the countries concerned, and by way of example some were outlined: problems of race, the influence of great powers, consequences of underdevelopment, and others. It was suggested that precision in defining relationships would suggest means of cooperation in dealing with problems faced in common. Then it went on:

> Assuming the perception of persistent common problems, and possible avenues of cooperation in meeting them, a next step would be to tackle the matter of mutual images, that is the perception each party has of the others. In relation to this, scholars can make a contribution by stating general theories, that is by stating what appear to them to be common motivations and objectives of all states. The comparison between the images scholars have of states, and the images states have of each other, might assist both scholars and the parties to the dispute to come to a closer approximation of reality.
>
> Finally, and again provided there is a basis of agreement at each successive step, consideration might be given to means of consultation and communication between parties to the dispute, even while the dispute is in progress – even while there may be armed clashes. This involves some consideration of 'de-escalation' and the re-establishment of communications as a means to the settlement of the dispute, rather than waiting upon the settlement of the dispute.

In December 1965 the nominees of the three governments met in London in the presence of ten scholars. The government nominees were senior officials attached to London diplomatic missions and other persons nominated by responsible Ministers. Usually each party was represented by two persons. At the end of the first week officials of two other governments were invited to join the discussions, at the suggestion of the parties directly involved. The scholars included two political scientists professionally engaged in the study of international relations, three social psychologists, two industrial relations specialists, an international lawyer, a regional historian, and a chairman with long experience in the conduct of small meetings.

The preparatory work, apart from a visit to the countries concerned and a general study of the problems of each, included the preparation of a set of propositions drawn from the theoretical literature that seemed to be relevant to this conflict. These were discussed by a wider group of social and political scientists at a seminar. The intention was that during the course of discussions attention would be drawn to these to test their relevance and validity, and to see in what ways they should be modified. While no agenda was prepared the procedures contemplated were:

(*a*) to obtain a statement of the situation as perceived by each party, and to obtain elaborations as seemed necessary to satisfy theoretical interests;

(*b*) to deduce the general political framework in which the states operated (for example, a fear-framework due to internal tensions and external intervention);

(*c*) to direct attention to specific causes of fear, means of removing them, means of promoting a sense of internal and external security;

(*d*) to seek from each party, in the light of the theoretical framework that emerged, the requests it would make on the others, and on states outside the region, and the steps towards normal relations it would be prepared to take unilaterally, or as part of a reciprocal pattern;

(*e*) to make a schedule of these requests, and to examine

them to ensure that they dealt with the basic features
of the conflict-situation;

(*f*) to submit a schedule of requests to all interested
parties for their comment;

(*g*) to isolate any requests that were unacceptable to
others, and re-examine their value to the parties
making them, and costs to the parties to which they
were made, and to prepare another schedule;

(*h*) to continue this process until a wholly agreed
schedule was obtained, and

(*i*) to invite states concerned to act unilaterally in
accordance with this schedule of requests, without
further negotiation, agreement or public statement,
as from an agreed date.

These seemed reasonable procedures. In practice they
turned out to be too rigid. Within a few days it became
apparent that the scholars around the table were directing
rather than controlling the communication of the parties.
Social psychologists tended quickly to diagnose the root
causes of conflict and to impose their models on the basis
of group relationships they thought were analogous, the
international lawyer was intent upon drafting heads of
agreement, and the political scientists tended to divert
discussion to the relationships that seemed particularly significant to them. It was the good sense and understanding
of the parties, and furthermore their desire to help to solve
their problems, that gave the scholars time to reassess and
to alter their tactics and approaches. The scholars became
more humble. Discussion by the parties very quickly
became less tied to formal positions, admissions were made
that motivations were mixed, fears not usually expressed
were explained and reasons given for them, and generally
the background conditions of conflict, internal and external, came to be revealed. In the process many of the

situations familiar to case workers were experienced. For example, the parties assisted each other in describing their problems, for the benefit of a group of ill-informed scholars, and the parties cooperated as well as communicated in the analysis of their common problems. The fact of the conflict receded into the background as the problem to be solved was more clearly defined. Alternative means of attaining the same objectives without the costs of conflict and by various means of cooperation were finally discussed. Reports were made back to diplomatic missions and governments as seemed to be required. At the end of the first week discussions were less frequent, but communication continued by these means over several months as and when it was considered some useful purpose would be fulfilled.

This was a pilot project. Much was learned about the degree to which scholars could usefully carry on their own theoretical discussions, the degree to which reference could be made to seemingly analogous situations, to which reference could be made to conditions within each state that might have a bearing on foreign relations, to which the conflict under discussion could be modelled, and to which knowledge in related areas of study could be applied to conflict between states. The impressive lesson was that in analysis and in resolution of conflict it was communication between the parties that was instructive and effective. Scholars had an important role in injecting new information, and in other ways helping the parties to stand back from their conflict so as to see it as a problem to be solved; but it was the controlled communication of the parties that was valuable. It was not useful for the third party to impose or even to suggest interpretations, explanations or remedies. It was in the light of this pilot study that the term 'controlled communication' was introduced to describe the technique.

In 1966 a second discussion took place, this time with two parties involved in a communal conflict that was of international concern. The level of representation was similar, the representatives having been nominated by the leaders of the parties in conflict. Three scholars from the United States, Professors C. F. Alger, H. C. Kelman and R. C. North, assisted members of the Centre, and more care was given to procedures than had previously been possible. In particular a more deliberate attempt was made to set down theoretically-derived propositions, and preliminary seminar discussion took place on the basis of these. The following is an extract from the document prepared for preparatory seminar discussion. References to the situation being discussed have been eliminated, but the propositions will indicate the analytical framework in which the particular conflict was considered. In the event it was found that these propositions served as a useful guide to discussion.

The processes by which one analyses an actual situation of conflict seem to be the following. One obtains some general impressions from reading (e.g. press reports, mediators' reports) and discussion (e.g. with those who have had first-hand experience). This information is accepted within a personal framework of knowledge of politics, of sociological studies, and of prejudices of all kinds. One visits and perceives, and the situation unfolds within this framework of prior personal experience, and the further personal experience of conversation with and entertainment by the parties to the dispute and subjective judgements as to motivations.

The next step is to set down the questions that are prompted by this experience. In addition, as a check against personal prejudice, one sets down the questions that are prompted by other work done in the field of conflict, for example the propositions concerning conflict formulated by Simmel and Coser, and more recently by Campbell and Le Vine. There are, in addition, propositions suggested by work on political systems, communications, decision-making and other aspects of politics.

One will have selected propositions in a personal and prejudicial way, but it will be a wide selection. In practice, the hypotheses that are significant are few. The problem is objectively to find which they are.

Discussion with other analysts, some of whom may be more familiar with propositions of general application than with the actual situation, will lead to additions and deletions of propositions, and also to more refinement in exposition. Discussion with the parties to the dispute, and subsequent reconsideration by the analysts of their original propositions, should point to the significant ones.

The parties to the dispute could be asked directly the questions the analysts have in mind in relation to the situation. This procedure, however, would lead to prejudiced answers by one party, and refutations by the other. In order to obtain guidance toward significant propositions, it is necessary to induce as much objectivity as possible into observations made by the parties. While the academic framework provided by controlled communication itself helps to do this, it may be desirable to avoid direct questions, and to seek observations on propositions couched in general terms, which have an application in other situations.

It is to be anticipated that the parties will play down the significance of propositions that touch upon sensitive spots, and, in fact, deny their significance. One of the roles of members of the panel is to ensure that propositions that they think might be important are fully explored, but without pressing the parties too far on any one occasion. Again, the parties will ignore aspects, not because they wish to repress, but merely because they have not perceived them.

Below is a first attempt to set down the questions and propositions that seem to be relevant, though perhaps not in all cases significant.

1. A trend in world society is toward independence of unitary communities in decision-making, evidenced by the demands for independence from colonialism, and for autonomy within states once they become independent, and by resistance to foreign influences. Any reversed tendency, that is movements toward stable federal structures or unions, is a development based upon already integrated units each having like political structures and social values.

2. States are political systems operating within an environment of other systems to which they are adapting and responding: 'national interests' are not fixed goals and include these adaptive processes.

3. Because states not involved attach value to their independence, they are more inclined to favour decisions willingly arrived at between parties to disputes than settlements imposed upon them; provided the parties have taken into account the legitimate interests of others, their agreements will attract support in world councils and in world consensus.

4. Law and order as maintained by colonial or foreign rule consolidates conflict situations, inhibits the flow of adjustments between communities, and thus creates situations of open conflict once authority is withdrawn.

5. The requirements of law and order lead colonial administrations to enlist the support of élites. These, because of their official positions and foreign support, tend to move away from the people whom they are supposed to represent and to govern, and this leads to increased tensions between the colonial administration and the people, as well as between the élites and the people.

6. Where the colonial administration employs members of one faction for police or administrative duties, because of their greater loyalty or special abilities, and in circumstances in which the administration faces unrest or independence demands, this faction is identified with the administration, and communal conflict is created even where none previously existed. This

communal conflict is likely to be exaggerated by transference processes, and to outlast the independence fighting.

7. Leadership interests result in statements that exaggerate conflict, and actions that raise its intensity. Ultimately leadership may be forced to maintain open conflict by contrived situations and propaganda, as a precaution against loss of enthusiasm.

8. A settlement of a conflict cannot always resolve it, and resolution may depend upon long-term policies. For a settlement to lead to resolution it must not contain elements of separateness, and must contain the basis of integration, especially in respect of educational policies and constitutional provisions.

9. Parties to a dispute should not be required to compromise.

The tensions and hostility were higher at the opening of these discussions than had been the case in the previous experience, but the general course and nature of discussions were similar. Partly because of lessons learned and partly because of greater general knowledge amongst scholars participating, control was exercised within twenty-four hours in ways outlined in subsequent chapters, and discussions were more in respect of a problem to be solved than in respect of the on-going conflict. Misperceptions, false interpretations of official statements, prejudice between national groups, unrealistic expectations about the policies of other states, and many other such relevant causes of misunderstanding and inaccurate calculation were revealed. It was possible to bring to bear with greater effect than in the previous exercise research findings on conflict, conflict escalation and conflict resolution.

These experiences stimulated various hypotheses about the nature of conflict, and also about processes of conflict resolution. Series of discussions were subsequently undertaken with representatives of governments involved in conflict so as to explore some of these further. Visits were made to two areas of conflict. Studies were made of other conflict situations with the assistance of diplomatic representatives in London.

Some of the matters that have been separately studied as a result of these experiences are: the extent to which international conflict has its origins in internal or communal conflict, patterns in attitudes and misperceptions commonly held, processes of escalation of conflict, conditions in which parties are and are not prepared to subject themselves to this kind of examination, the possibilities of conflict avoidance by means of controlled communication, the reaction of practitioners to academic enquiry into their affairs, and problems of mediation that occur when parties are not brought together face-to-face. Some of these are dealt with in an assessment of the value of controlled communication in the second Part of this study.

2   Conflicts, Parties and Issues

The bringing together of representatives of parties to a conflict in the presence of a panel of political scientists, and the application of supportive approaches as have been developed in social casework, are merely the consequences of, or the procedures that are suggested by, contemporary insistence upon greater precision in analysis. The technique itself is the logical extension of detailed analysis by which a total situation is broken down into component parts for purposes of examination, and of recent theoretical thinking that has tended to direct increased attention to systems of interactions within and among nations and states. An analytical approach requires the identification of the parties to any conflict in relation to the issues that are in dispute between them. Anyone studying conflicts is aware that many states can be found to be parties to a dispute because of the interactions that take place in world society. The act of bringing parties together in a face-to-face small-group discussion, however, necessitates decisions as to which are primarily concerned, and which parties are interested in particular issues.

(i) THE IDENTIFICATION OF PARTIES

At first sight the identification of the parties to a conflict might seem to be a straightforward procedure, and one that has always been followed in traditional approaches to the peaceful settlement of conflict. Whenever there is a dispute there are, by definition, parties to it. Rarely, however, is it straightforward. We have tended to think it is because we have become accustomed to descriptive accounts of conflicts and situations of tension that lump together the parties on each side. Every international problem or situation of conflict has appeared to be one involving one group of states and interests on one side, and another on the other. The two world wars were fought between two groups of states each in a wartime alliance. Traditional mediation reflects this approach. For example, the Security Council in its resolution of 4 March 1964 regarded the governments of Greece, Turkey and the United Kingdom, and the two communities in Cyprus, as parties to a dispute. A mediator was appointed by the Secretary-General with the task of finding a solution acceptable to all.

The implication in the grouping together of parties is that a solution of an international problem depends upon agreement between the two groups of states that are in conflict. But this is misleading. Parties to a dispute are not all equally involved, nor are they concerned with the same issues. No solution is likely to be found that would satisfy all the parties involved. After cessation of hostilities in the Second World War attempts were made to arrange settlements between the two groups as though each were a unified alliance in which the members had common values and interests. But the victorious allies could not agree on peace terms: different interests were revealed, and it became clear that the war had been fought over different issues. In the Cyprus case the mediator finally came to the conclusion that the two communities should meet together as a first step towards an overall solution.[1] It was not one dispute. The two communities were in dispute over issues that were at the down-to-earth level of personal political participation and non-discrimination. There were other disputes that involved different parties and different issues. There was the dispute between the Greek and Turkish Governments, and the issues were their defence requirements and traditional prestige considerations in relation to Cyprus. They might have been purporting to be acting on behalf of and in defence of the communities; but their own negotiations and activities indicated that their interests were not firstly those of the local communities. There was another dispute between the United States of America and the Soviet Union – not mentioned in the Security Council resolution as parties – and the United Kingdom was also interested. The issues relevant to all three were related to global strategy. No compromise or solution could be found by a mediator to satisfy all of these varied interests. Ultimately, if a solution were to be found, face-to-face discussion was required first of all at the level of the communities, and at other levels only in respect of issues in dispute between parties at these levels, as, for example, those arising as a consequence of any agreement reached at the local level. The reasons why a solution finally depends upon resolution at the ground level is suggested below.

To take another example, the Rhodesian situation was dealt with by the United Nations, at the request of the United Kingdom, as 'a problem' – undefined except that a white minority was defying Britain and exercising an unlawful, and to the United Nations, an unacceptable jurisdiction over an African majority. The parties to one dispute were the United Kingdom government and the *de facto* government of Rhodesia. These were the parties represented at negotiations on HMS *Tiger* in 1966. The issues were constitutional ones relevant to British powers. The parties to another dispute were the United Nations and the *de facto* government. Other parties in conflict over other issues were the European and the African communities. The European community in Rhodesia was broadly represented by the *de facto* government, but the African community could not as readily be identified. Perhaps owing to continued repression, the banning of parties and the gaoling of leaders, the African community was sharply divided between ZANU and ZAPU, and even these parties may not have represented African thinking. Bitterness between these two parties was at least as great as between each of them and the Europeans.[2] Nor were the precise issues clear: the African one-man–one-vote demand, and the European demand for continued privilege, were not sufficiently precise as issues to determine whether the communities could be represented for purposes of negotiation or peaceful settlement.[3]

These two cases are typical of other situations: rarely is there only one dispute. In the Indonesian–Malaysian confrontation there were many disputes and issues, ranging from basic ethnic and community ones (Malays being the dominant group in each state) to those concerning the three governments, and to others of wider international interest. So, too, with Suez, Cuba, Israel and other situations of conflict.

A problem may be the sum total of a series of disputes, and be referred to as such as an historical event; but for purposes of analysis and resolution each sub-dispute requires separate treatment. It could be argued that they must be lumped together because political realism finally dictates the dominance of greater powers. It is more likely that it is failure to separate out the parties and issues that gives a problem an appearance of complexity that requires some external coercive settlement. It is probable that it is failure to resolve conflicts at the local level that leads to influences from other levels.

The reasons for the existence of different disputes within the one conflict are now becoming clearer. More recent approaches to the study of international relations have emphasised the degree to which international conflict is a spill-over from internal or communal strife. Parties within a state seek outside assistance, and other states, sometimes with different interests to pursue and frequently without full knowledge of the reasons for the internal conflict or the consequences of their intervention, are usually ready to intervene. Thus the local dispute becomes a matter of international concern.[4] Internal or communal strife usually refers to conflict between racial, religious and cultural groups. However, analytically ideological or political conflict within a state can be regarded as communal conflict, including cases of severe economic dislocation that lead to aggressive policies, as was the case with Hitler's Germany. Sociologists might see internal tensions as a source of United States fears of communism, and therefore a source of United States policies of intervention in political disputes in Latin American and Asian states.[5] In many cases there is an interaction process which leads some states to intervene, for domestic reasons, in the affairs of others, and for the governments of states so penetrated to welcome this foreign intervention, for their own reasons. Communal conflict, therefore, is associated in one way or another with a wide variety, and a high proportion, of international conflicts, giving rise to many disputes within the one conflict situation.

There is a widespread presumption in political writings that states seek their independence from foreign influence and intervention, which would suggest that this spill-over is not general. But the empirical evidence is that since 1945 many states have invited intervention in one form or another. Immediately after the Second World War European states competed for United States financial assistance by claiming internal communist threats, and in Asia and Latin America many governments sought foreign military support. Governments that are legitimised seek independence from foreign influence, but governments that do not enjoy a legitimised status seek intervention. The Cold War may be looked upon at some future point in history as being a function of social and political change within states rather than a simple power rivalry between the United States of America and the Soviet Union. Clearly any resolution of such an extended conflict must finally be based upon an agreement at the domestic level; agreement among the states that were invited to participate, and which accepted the invitation because of their own interests, could not resolve the original problem. Vietnam was evidence of this.

(ii) SYSTEMS LEVELS

It is useful at this point to introduce the concept of systems levels and to explain why it is that conflict must be resolved at one level before there can be resolution at others.

Above we broke the Cyprus and Rhodesian problems down into disputes at the local level and at levels involving foreign parties. The different disputes within one problem may for convenience be regarded as disputes at different systems levels. The concept of system helps to explain the nature of a problem as a whole, and the disputes which comprise it. Systems are transactions between units of the same set. The two communities in Cyprus were one set, the governments of Greece and Turkey another.

It will at once be clear that the transactions that are most numerous, intimate and persistent, are those at the local level. It is disruption of these that creates conflict, and it is restoration of these that resolves it. A settlement arrived at by governments at other systems levels and imposed at the local level does not necessarily, and in practice is unlikely to, restore transactions at the local level.

This general proposition requires qualification. The division of North and South Korea severed transactions and established new ones, creating new systems. Parts of these new systems would be destroyed by a reunification. This may happen in due course. The point is made only that when a conflict leads to severance of transactions the resolution of conflict is less dependent upon resolution at local systems levels.

The general proposition is, therefore, that the starting point in analysis and resolution of conflict is at the systems level of highest transactions. A settlement imposed from other levels could occur, as for example after military defeat of one side. It could even lead to resolution; but only after a sufficiently long period of time, and by procedures that ensured the severance of past transactions and the building of new systems. Presumably this is what the United States sought to do in Vietnam in preference to resolution on the basis of discussions at the local level. The systems or transactions concept helps to demonstrate the options open in a given situation, and the different problems involved in resolution by re-establishing transactions at local levels, on the one hand, and settlement or resolution by creating new systems, on the other.

(iii) DIVISION WITHIN PARTIES

Not only has there been a tendency to lump together

states into one party to a dispute; there has also been a tendency to assume that each state or faction is a unified whole, and that its members have a common attitude to the dispute in question. It has been assumed that the interests of a state in an alliance, or of a state acting alone, can be represented by the government of that state, and that agreements entered into will be observed. A further implication is that conflicts between states are conflicts of interests between the peoples of states. It is true – with some qualifications made below – that once violence takes place and there is a threat to a state, a high degree of internal unity takes place: interest in survival tends to outweigh all other values. But it is not true that states are unified in their values or can be represented completely by governments. In reality, states in conflict are typically not unified internally.[6] At best governments are never wholly legitimised. On the contrary they frequently represent minority viewpoints. Australia refused to recognise China in 1949, despite a wide consensus in favour, because a Labour government tried to satisfy a minority faction within its own ranks immediately prior to an election.[7] In Vietnam, one of the main reasons why the military government refused to have discussions with the National Liberation Front or in any way to recognise it as a decision-making entity was that it itself had no legitimised status, and that substantial proportions of its electorate were in favour of a negotiated settlement. In-fighting in Israel, the United Arab Republic, the United States of America in relation to Vietnam, and in almost all states involved in situations of national concern, conditions behaviour and policies.

It follows that there cannot be resolution of conflict and a stable condition unless there is a high degree of internal unity of purpose, and even then instability or rejection of agreements can occur through changes in values and interests. It also follows that the origins of conflict, those interests and values the state is pursuing or defending, may not be the interests and values of groups and factions within states, and perhaps not even the interests and values of majorities. It follows, also, that conflict avoidance is possible only when means are found by which interests and values can be assessed by the parties with full knowledge of the costs of conflict in relation to the values being pursued, and of interests and values being destroyed by it.

Divisions within parties are an important cause of escalation of conflict. Statements and policies designed to satisfy political extremists, and to divert attention to foreign scapegoats during periods of economic failure and political disruption, are a familiar feature of international politics. Such statements and policies of one state are made in an international environment that includes many other states facing the same problems of internal disunity, and reacting in the same way. The aggressive statements of one state justify the policies of another, and an escalation of conflict is initiated that has no foundation other than domestic struggles for economic and social reform, and the more mundane struggles for party political power. It seems that China interpreted official and unofficial statements made in Washington over Formosa as a threat, whereas they had a domestic purpose, and having responded accordingly, unwittingly gave support to the factions in the United States that were advocating aggressive policies.

Escalated conflict in due course accentuates internal divisions: costs in relation to values become clearer. It has frequently been assumed that 'threat causes in-group solidarity'.[8] The proposition refers to situations in which a group is forced to push to one side its internal differences in the face of serious external dangers. 'The exigencies of war with outsiders are what make peace inside, lest internal discord should weaken the one group for war.'[9] This is an over-simplification that tends to cloud over an important cause of conflict. In practice, an outside threat might lead to in-group solidarity when the threat is of limited duration, and can be met effectively by in-group solidarity. If, however, it continues over long periods, and attempts to meet it are frustrated, in-group conflict results, and the more aggressive parties achieve control. Japan before the Second World War struggled to attain sources of materials and markets for manufactured products. When moderate policies had no pay-off, when the protectionist policies of Western states seemed to be institutionalised, internal divisions occurred that resulted in a military élite deciding to force the issues. China was integrated in its opposition to United States policies of containment, and in its response to exclusion from world councils. Years of frustration led to internal division between 'moderates' willing to follow policies calculated to present an image of China that conformed, despite provocations, and those, on the other hand, who saw no possibility of China breaking Western policies other than by continued revolution outside as well as inside China. Far from threat promoting integration, it can be disintegrative, and furthermore, ultimately a cause of aggressive responses.

Consideration of unit integration directs attention to the points within a political system that require attention: a resolution of a conflict between two states cannot be superimposed upon continuing conflicts within them. Problems of unit integration arise out of problems of alienation, of participation in decision-making, of leadership and élite interests. In the Asian cases they frequently relate to land tenure systems, forms of feudal government, the absence of social and economic opportunities. Provided change takes place slowly, and adjustment keeps pace with change, the unit remains integrated. In the normal course, leadership responds to demands made on it. If at any stage adjustment can be resisted by reason of an expectation of outside help, demands quickly become greater than adjustment capability. Outside help is then required, and escalated conflict occurs. Experience is that legal legitimacy is deprived of sociological legitimacy by the failure of ruling élites to meet demands made on them, this failure being due to promises of foreign assistance. The resulting conflict cannot be settled by outside force; it can be resolved only by regaining unit integration.

The virtue of controlled communication is that it is based upon face-to-face discussion in which persons have to represent a viewpoint, thus forcing upon states a need to clarify their own thinking, and more importantly, forcing upon each party a recognition that the conflict relates to internal problems on both sides which have to be understood, if not solved, before there can be any measure of agreement. From the point of view of analysis, it draws attention to the possibility that international conflict is in reality a problem, not of international organisation and repression of aggression, but of internal political organisation within states. The seeds of conflict are probably not within the international system; they may be found within the decision-making processes of states.

(iv) IDENTIFICATION OF ISSUES

It cannot be assumed that the issues as perceived by the parties to be those in dispute are those at the source of conflict. In so far as the origins of conflict are within states, and within factions in states, and in so far as other states become involved, the issues are likely to be both mis-stated and confused. At no stage was there in the United States or elsewhere in the Western world any agreed view of what were the issues in conflict in Vietnam.

There are many reasons why this is so, apart from the usual absence of analytical separation of parties and issues. First, the issues in conflict are not clear to the parties themselves. Hitler's conflict with the allies could have had its origins in mass unemployment and social unrest, which could be traced to the consequences of the First World War. The allies saw nazism as a threat to their security, but nazism could have been a product of the circumstances of Germany, and the removal of the Nazi party might not have altered events. At a certain stage the issue for the Western allies was survival. Second, whatever might be the issues originally, they tend to be pushed into the background as conflict escalates. In Vietnam the original issues related to the interests and values of a feudal government. Soon the issue was perceived by the West as one of communist, if not Chinese, expansion. Third, events that finally lead to conflict are often merely ones that trigger it, and not the underlying reasons for it, as when a Turkish policeman was shot in Cyprus.

Even in cases of communal conflict it is not always clear that the origins of conflict relate to the presence of different ethnic groups. The same kinds of conflict emerge between different classes within the same ethnic group. Fear and threat, denial of participation rights, perceived injustice, disappointment in expectations, are the typical origins of conflict behaviour: it is the specific causes of these, including misperceptions of the environment, that are the issues in conflict.

In practice the issues relevant to the resolution of conflict require a search into the motivations and perceptions of the parties, and part of the purpose of controlled communication is to identify them. Little more can be done in advance of discussions than to determine issues in broad terms so as to separate them according to systems levels. It is clear that local issues are different from those over which states that intervene are in conflict; but it is not clear in advance what precisely are these issues. Issues and parties must be matched. Parties around a table in an unstructured discussion themselves determine some issues, and others are brought to the surface by questions from the third party.

(v) INVITATIONS

The parties invited to discuss their conflicts in a controlled setting were those that appeared in each case to be the ones most concerned with transactions affected or disrupted by the conflicts, and not necessarily those expending on the conflicts the greatest quantities of men and resources, or those who might have claimed to have an interest in the conflicts. As discussions proceeded and issues of wider significance appeared to be relevant, other parties were approached. This is the reverse of traditional practices: the great powers have been among the first states to discuss local disputes and to be consulted by mediators. Whatever might have been the position in the past, great powers are rarely in sufficient agreement to be in a position to settle the disputes of others. In any event, the settlement of their conflicts by other states is no longer acceptable to independent nations that in the contemporary world society insist upon determining their own values and interests.

Even the parties that were invited to discussions were found not to be unified: they included factions with different values and interests, and frequently discussion of these was relevant. In some cases it was found impossible to identify parties, and therefore impossible to invite any in relation to a conflict which without doubt existed. A far longer process of controlled communication at systems levels below the national one was relevant. The leaders of some of the parties in these cases are often under detention or in other ways not available, as was the case in Rhodesia.

NOTES TO CHAPTER TWO

(1) See UN Security Council documents S/6253, p. 65.
(2) See Shamuyarira, *Crisis in Rhodesia*, ch. 10.
(3) As part of the research programme of the Centre for the Analysis of Conflict some consideration was given to this problem, and a submission was made in 1967 to the Rhodesian Constitutional Commission. Extracts from the text are contained in an appendix to this chapter.
(4) See, for example, Denton, 'Some Regularities in International Conflict, 1820–1949', pp. 283–96; Modelski, 'The International Relations of Internal War', pp. 14–43; and Luard, *Conflict and Peace in the Modern International System*.
(5) See Burton, 'Western Intervention in South East Asia'.
(6) See companion study, ch. 3.
(7) See Albinski, *Australian Policies and Attitudes towards China*.
(8) Campbell, *Ethnocentric and Other Altruistic Motives*, p. 288.
(9) W. G. Sumner, quoted by Campbell, ibid. p. 289.

APPENDIX TO CHAPTER TWO*

THE RHODESIAN CONSTITUTIONAL PROBLEM

Extracts from a submission by the Director of the Centre for the Analysis of Conflict, University College London,

* See note 3. above

to the Rhodesian Constitutional Commission, Salisbury, April 1967.

What the Centre is doing in relation to communal and international conflict is what has been done in recent years in relation to industrial and small-group conflict where judicial settlements are not appropriate. The judicial function is relevant where interpretation of law is required, or where settlement can be imposed by a legitimised authority. But industrial, family, communal and international conflicts involve values and attitudes, and an imposed settlement usually provokes aggressive responses, either immediately or at a later stage. Judicial procedures, and even conciliation and mediation, do not lead parties to reperceive the dispute itself, and the behaviour of each other, which is necessary for a resolution – as distinct from a settlement – of the dispute. On the contrary, quasi-judicial processes and formal negotiations such as diplomatic exchanges and negotiations between community leaders, frequently serve to reinforce attitudes. Controlled communication of the type the Centre has evolved seems to result in altered attitudes and perceptions, and even on some occasions, to a re-assessment of values in relation to the costs of the conflict.

We have interested ourselves in the Rhodesian problem as part of our research activities. We would have liked to have arranged the same type of controlled communication that we have arranged in other cases as a means of analysing the problem. But to have done this would have required the precise identification of the parties involved, and their representatives. At one systems level the parties are the United Kingdom and the Rhodesian governments, or the United Nations and the Rhodesian government. From our point of view these parties, and the issues discussed between them, are not the relevant ones. Resolution of conflict – as distinct from enforced settlement – is possible only at the local or basic systems levels. At these levels we have not been able satisfactorily to identify either the parties or the precise issues which are in conflict. However, it might be possible to use the analyses we have already made of other communal conflicts at least to put forward some basic propositions in the framework of which this particular problem can be considered. This might enable a more objective approach to the problem by the communities concerned. In any event, a constitutional approach to a political problem can succeed in the longer term only to the degree to which constitutional provisions reflect an accurate analysis of the problem and of the felt needs of those concerned. A second contribution we might make is in relation to procedures: provisions put forward as a result of some procedures might be unacceptable to some factions concerned, while the same provisions put forward in another context might be acceptable. It needs to be stressed that this is a research Centre. It has no contribution to make in determining goals and values; these are for the parties to determine. Nor can it suggest to parties the precise details of means to be adopted in resolving a problem, which must take into account local conditions of which we have little knowledge.

THE NATURE OF COMMUNAL CONFLICT

There is a tendency for parties involved in communal conflicts to regard their particular struggle as unique, and due largely to the special attributes of those who oppose them. The Chinese and Malays in Malaysia, the Fijians and Indians in Fiji, the Greek and Turkish Cypriots in Cyprus, and the Hindus and Moslems in India, feel themselves involved in special situations. In face-to-face discussions parties to a conflict at first resent other situations being used as part of the analysis of their own; but in due course they become interested in the similarities, especially in the ways in which conflicts escalate, and the images parties have of each other. Those studying conflict are aware of many patterns of behaviour that are common. National and communal leaders when first approached with the suggestion of face-to-face discussions make accusations about their opponents in terms identical with those their opponents use. In each case there is one party that considers itself more efficient, or more strongly backed by historical, legal and moral claims, and usually there is one party that is the more energetic and another that feels itself threatened or exploited. Indeed, in the study of communal conflicts it is hard to make any clear-cut distinctions even between various types of communal conflict. On the surface some appear to be racial, some religious, some ideological within the one ethnic group, and many are combinations of these. Conflict in Rhodesia, Malaysia and Fiji is racial on the surface. In Cyprus this is not so, yet most of the basic features of all these conflicts are the same. Moreover, these communal conflicts do not differ fundamentally from a widespread form of communal conflict, class conflict. In every case there are groups that feel themselves excluded from decision-making, exploited, discriminated against, and groups that feel they have some special rights derived from history, law, moral values, energy and intelligence.

Most states comprise different communities. If religion and class are regarded as forms of communal conflict, then every state faces communal problems in some form. It is instructive to examine those in which the problem has been resolved by political and constitutional procedures. The more unified states are the older ones: in each there has been a long process of social and political struggle. In Britain it is only since the Second World War that educational and occupational opportunities have been generally available, and there still remain pockets of privilege. The egalitarian welfare state is a recent development. Race accentuates the problem of social unification, and in Britain there is now widespread discrimination against non-European immigrants – despite government measures to prevent it. The immigrants form an additional pool of underprivileged, and it will be a long process before they achieve equality of opportunities. There are few short cuts in the resolution of class or communal conflict.

The problem is to find and take advantage of any that are practical.

In some rare cases a minority succeeds in securing and preserving its interests more quickly than is usually possible, and still within a constitutional framework. For example, in Australia Roman Catholics comprise one-fifth of the population. Their interests include government support for their own educational establishments, and many provisions in domestic and foreign policies. They can secure these interests thanks to their political organisation, and to their existence as a third political force in a balance of power position. This is a rare case. The 'democratic' party political system usually ensures that any minority of less than fifty per cent is unrepresented in any effective party. It works smoothly only in communities in which political parties are not greatly divided on religious, ethnic, cultural or ideological grounds, as is the case in Britain and the United States of America. Even in these cases it is not clear that it is desirable to have up to fifty per cent of the community not represented in a government. Wherever there is a nation in which there are communities with greatly differing values or interests, and minorities that can only be permanent parliamentary oppositions, the one-man–one-vote principle is likely to operate unjustly.

Where the underprivileged community is a politically ineffective minority, as is the case in Britain, the majority can accommodate it, and even legislate for the protection of its interests. The slow process of integration can take place. This is a very slow process where racial minorities are concerned. Where the minority is a politically effective one, because of its size, its economic role or its foreign support, a conflict situation is likely, as in the case of Cyprus.

Where the underprivileged community is a majority, the minority can be expected to try to deny electoral opportunities to the majority, and the majority to demand one-man–one-vote. This is the position in Fiji, and will be in Malaysia. The minority can maintain its position only by coercion and threatened force, and by guarantees by foreign states, thereby inviting an internal power response, and intervention by other foreign states. These particular situations are sources of serious international conflict, but the communities are fairly evenly balanced in numbers and conditions of life, and these conditions serve to give time for adjustments.

The situation in Rhodesia is of this type, with the difference that the minority is very small, and has a much-envied, very high comparative living standard. It retains its position by a virtual monopoly of political and military power. Not even the level of political participation and cooperation as exists in the more typical cases of Malaysia and Fiji can be contemplated by the minority. Consequently, not even that slow process of integration, or the measure of coexistence, hoped for in these other cases, can be anticipated by the African majority in Rhodesia. The motivations on each side are compelling: the one side tends to adopt the all-or-nothing policy of minority rule supported by military power, and the other tends to hold to unqualified majority rule by electoral power.

POLITICAL ANALYSIS

Before turning to alternatives, some reference to the political processes involved needs to be made.

There are three sets of values that are pursued simultaneously in any political system: the political values of those who seek or occupy positions of authority; group values, only some of which are represented by those in these political positions; and national values that are common to all. The political process is such that authorities act to preserve themselves, and the interests they represent. Other organised group interests come second, and national interests tend to be interpreted in the light of political and group pressures. Wherever there are marked differences in interests within a political system there is at least some loss of political support for authorities, and sometimes organised opposition. In this situation there is a reduced level of legitimisation of authority. The presence of legitimised authority, that authority which rests upon the support of those over whom it is being exercised without reliance upon threat or coercion, is the test of the presence of politically acceptable levels of participation in the political process. There can be very low levels of participation, and yet an acceptance of authority (at least for a time), as is the case when there is strong leadership in new states. Sociological legitimacy leads to legal legitimacy, but cannot be equated with it. Legal legitimacy is frequently obtained by force, and even though it might originally be derived from sociological processes, sometimes it is maintained by force. It will be at once obvious that the form of authority, and the means by which power is attained, are not tests of legitimisation: the test is the degree of support authorities receive, measured by electoral processes, by the absence of protest, or by the absence of any need for coercive restraints. Whatever the political process involved in the filling of positions of authority – electoral, military, hereditary or any other – authorities have or have not a high legitimised status according to the degree to which they reflect the values existing within the political system. Legitimisation of authority rests upon performance in the satisfaction of values, and not upon the political processes of attaining office.

It follows that it is not the existence of different communities that leads to conflict between them, but the failure of the political system to satisfy demands. When, in any political system, the demands of one community are satisfied, and others perceive discrimination by authorities against them, there is a condition of communal conflict. This is clearly demonstrable in cases such as Cyprus, Malaysia, Fiji and Rhodesia, where government is dominated by one of the communities comprising the political system. In such conditions, even attempts not to discriminate are likely to be misinterpreted, merely because full and equitable participation has been denied to some sections of the society.

A community within a state system that is not satisfied that its legitimate demands are being met, has three choices: the seeking of guarantees against discrimination, violence or revolution to gain control, partition or separate organisation. All three are likely to involve seeking foreign assistance. Whether the community or faction is a religious, ethnic or political one makes little difference; there are likely to be other states, or communities and factions in other states, that have an interest in responding to appeals for assistance. Any general condition of unrest and lack of popular support for a government is likely to give rise to appeals for foreign assistance, and finally to conflict that is international.

Participation not being the fundamental consideration, the solution to these problems is not necessarily the procedure of one-man–one-vote. Under such a system Turkish Cypriots, Malays and Fijians would feel themselves prejudiced and threatened. There is no principle involved in relation to one-man–one-vote: it is a Western system that has been found to be unsuited to the needs of developing states. In the typical Western federal system the procedure is not followed. There are two legislative bodies, one on a one-man–one-vote basis, and the other on a regional basis, each separate region having the same voting strength regardless of its size and its numbers. The Australian Commonwealth Parliament is organised in this way—each state has the same number of representatives in the Senate, regardless of size.

However, attempts to construct alternatives to one-man–one-vote processes have rarely met with success. In Malaysia and Fiji constitutional safeguards to preserve the interests of the Malays and Fijians, who are becoming a minority, have been provided, and there is reason to believe that they will prove to be self-defeating – they are, in practice, prejudicing the position of those whom they were designed to protect. An elaborate constitutional arrangement was introduced as a solution to the Cyprus dispute, and the provisions designed to protect the interests of the Turks seemed to render the constitution unworkable – at least in the view of the Greek Cypriots – and the consequent fighting threatened the welfare and lives of the Turks.

The reason for these failures is that the constitutions were drafted to give power to some groups, and protection to others against this power. They failed to take into account the psychological and sociological fact that the power-protection system increases suspicions, antagonism and conflict between communities because of the discriminations and uncertainties involved. The Malays are sensitive to the fact that they need protection, and the Chinese bear a grudge against the Malays which they did not have previously. Discrimination deliberately introduced for purposes of protection destroys social relationships as effectively as unofficial discrimination. In the Rhodesian situation Africans would resent protection against European political power, Europeans could not conceive of effective protection against African political power, and in any event, a power protection relationship does not provide any sound basis for communal cooperation.

ALTERNATIVES

Political stability is a condition in which the government is both sociologically and legally legitimate. For this to occur the felt needs and interests of the population must be met by the state, and an ideological, ethnical and cultural identity must develop, so that both law and the state are supported as ends in themselves. There is little difficulty in achieving this condition when the population is unified ethnically and ideologically.

In any state with two or more antipathetic ethnic or cultural communities, special problems occur. Where the communities are geographically separate the obvious solution is partition. In the contemporary world very small states can be politically and economically viable. But rarely is this the case. More often the different communities are intermingled geographically, and interdependent economically. Partition still must be considered; but in these cases it would be an extreme and desperate step, as was the case with India, involving contemporary suffering for many, and no firm prospect of future benefit or peaceful relationships between the two separated communities.

Some means, not including positive or negative discrimination, is required to enable each community to feel secure, and to maintain its values and traditions, and freely to cooperate with each other on a basis of equality in respect of matters of common interest. It would seem necessary to keep separate the organisation of ethnic and cultural values from the organisation of common needs and interests. Functional cooperation in the provision of common needs and interests is likely, in due course, to modify ethnic and cultural values, and to promote higher degrees of communal relationship.

This analysis implies separate legislatures for each ethnic group with powers in respect of agreed matters of special interest – such as religious ceremonies, traditional procedures of law and justice, local government and some aspects of education – and a common legislature with powers in respect of agreed matters of common interest – such as weights and measures, communications and defence. The former would each require tax powers relevant to their powers. To some degree this pattern once developed in Cyprus, and was traditional in Rhodesia.

Curiously enough the Rhodesian problem is made more, and not less, difficult by reason of the fact that the cultural patterns of the two communities have so much in common. The religious ceremonies and customs of the African people have already been greatly influenced by European administrations. There is less room for a clear-cut separation on racial lines of legislation dealing with marriage and education, as is the case in Cyprus. However, there are sufficient differences – subjective or objective – to justify this separation of legislative function, and the creation of two ethnically based legislatures, together with a common one. Furthermore, there are wider advantages in making possible the free development of separate cultures. Even if there were little justification on ethnic grounds for this legislative separation of ethnic and common interests, the constitutional arrangement would still be justified politically as a provisional arrangement. The separation of ethnic and special interests from the general interest could provide a transitional arrangement by which the felt needs of both communities could be met, provided adequate provisions were included for ultimate unification by progressive constitutional procedures.

There are few problems in the creation of ethnic legislatures, whether formal as in Cyprus, or unofficial as is the case with Roman Catholic control of behaviour relating to marriage and divorce. Where difficulties arise is in ensuring that the 'common needs and interests' function of the state will, in practice, cater for, and be seen by them to cater for, the ethnic needs of all communities. No community will be satisfied with a system controlled by another, regardless of domestic or foreign undertakings and guarantees against discrimination.

The difficulties are less daunting when the basis of representation is examined in the light of the powers and functions of the legislature concerned. When an administrative organisation or legislature has its powers confined to functional matters of common interest, representation and voting are less important. Unanimity is required for functional cooperation to succeed. International functional organisations dealing with communications, health and science operate smoothly despite equal representation of small and large states. Where there are two or more communities within a state they, no less, can be satisfied with equal representation, despite different numbers within them, on matters such as communications, weights and measures, minimum standards of health and education, and matters of this kind. The principle, therefore, is that the 'common needs and interests' legislature should be concerned only with those matters that are appropriate for consideration and decision on the basis of equal representation of communities.

In practice this system would lead to legislation by joint committees of investigation, and functional cooperation between representatives of communities with a professional interest in the subject matter – educational standards, medical care, and other specialised fields. A progressive expansion of powers given over by ethnic legislatures to the common needs and interest legislature, similar to the expansion of powers of federal legislatures, would ensure a progression towards greater functional cooperation between the communities.

In any federal system there is a need for some judicial authority to determine powers of legislatures. In an ethnic needs system a judicial authority would be required to exercise this function, and also the function of determining when seemingly discriminating practices were or were not within constitutional provisions. For instance, some discriminatory practices might be accepted in education conducted by ethnic authorities, but not in education conducted by the joint authorities.

Consideration of constitutional change on a continuous basis, and formal consideration by legislatures at the end of five-year periods, would provide a legitimised means of change to those who are dissatisfied. Change would require majorities in all legislatures.

PROCEDURES

The problem of Rhodesia is not merely or mainly constitutional. Ingenious schemes deliberately drafted to meet the needs of all parties could meet with violent resistance. First, they are unlikely to meet the needs of peoples not consulted, and second, even though they did, they would be rejected because of the absence of consultation.

In relation to the first, the presentation of suggestions on constitutional issues in respect of a particular problem was never contemplated as part of the work of this

Centre. On the contrary, we have held strictly to the
view that our function is to analyse conflicts, and it is
for the parties concerned to work toward their own
solutions, assisted by communication that we are able
to establish between them, and by the analysis we are
able to make during this communication. It is only the
parties that can reveal the values and fears involved,
and the many complexities of relationships. Constitutional solutions to communal problems have rarely done
more than postpone conflict. Objectives have been
determined as a matter of policy by one of the parties,
by a third party, or by constitutional lawyers, and not
from within the relationships concerned. Suggestions
from third parties, from commissions, from academics,
are likely to be proved unworkable when put to the
test, and to require support by coercion and threat, and
to fail in the longer term, unless checked at each stage
of consideration with the felt needs of the people
concerned.

In relation to the second, at best proposals can be a
basis for discussion, otherwise they become a determination – that is, a settlement rather than a resolution of a
conflict, with all manner of resistances developing in the
future. No constitutional approaches can succeed unless
all concerned are participants in their consideration.
In the situation as it has now developed, characterised
by unrealistic perceptions by the parties of each other,
not even miracle proposals that meet the declared needs
of all concerned would be acceptable, no matter who
put them forward. Each party now wants the certainty
of its own outright power dominance. It is only discussion of proposals, in adequately controlled conditions,
that can lead to reperceptions, to mutual appreciations
of fears and needs, and to the treatment of the situation
as a problem and not as a contest.

A constitutional convention, preferably academically
controlled, of representatives of every viewpoint seems
necessary, first to ensure objective needs are met, and
second to ensure that reperceptions take place to enable
an appreciation of objective needs. On the basis of our

own experience, and the history of disputes, we feel we cannot stress this procedural aspect too much: without face-to-face participation in the consideration of proposals, there can never take place the complex adjustments in attitudes and perceptions that is necessary for any set of proposals to succeed.

Consultation is possible in Rhodesia. The two prominent conflicting African parties may not be representative; they may even represent only extreme view-points. But a good test for a constitution is the reaction of extremists. Our own experience is that in a controlled situation, such as we have devised for research purposes, there are not extreme positions: extreme positions arise out of absence of participation and consultation, and the need to adopt bargaining positions, and to promote movements in support of direct action. Furthermore, experience is that divisions within ranks, such as have occurred within the African community, result from frustrations and differences in tactics, and not through any great differences in values and goals.

3 The Representatives of Parties

For there to be negotiation between parties to a dispute the parties must be capable of being represented: there can be no negotiation or communication with a party that is so diverse in its values, interests, goals and strategies as not to be able to agree to representatives.

Assuming that there is unity within the parties, the identification of persons who represent their views, attitudes and assumptions is no more straightforward than the identification of parties. In ordinary relations between states misunderstandings occur through the false identification of representatives, as when non-responsible members of a parliament are taken to represent the views of the government of the day. Even political leaders do not necessarily represent the views of their governments in their private or public statements. They speak to different audiences in different terms, they adopt bargaining positions, and they sometimes endeavour to deny the existence of policies that are already evolving.

For negotiation to lead to a lasting agreement the representatives must not only represent in a constitutional sense, but also reflect the views, and even the future views, of those they represent. Sometimes trade union officials arrive at agreements with managements that are later rejected by the rank and file. President Wilson failed to represent the views of the peoples of the United States as subsequently reflected in Congress.

Systems levels are clearly relevant to the identification of representatives. When an internal conflict has extended to include foreign states, a representative cannot be a spokesman both for the internal faction and for the foreign government that is in support of it. Different interests are involved. The United States regarded the government at Hanoi as the credible representative of the opposing forces; it would not initially agree to talks with the National Liberation Front, which was one of the parties relevant at the local level. Systems levels, parties, issues and representatives must all be relevant to each other.

Problems relating to representation are of two kinds, first those concerned with the actual selection of persons, and second those relating to effective communication between representatives and those they represent. These are especially important in the use of controlled communication.

(i) THE SELECTION OF REPRESENTATIVES

In the exercises so far carried out the representatives of governments have been nominated by the head of state or the responsible minister. It is only at this level that a decision can be taken whether to agree to meeting with other parties to a conflict. However, for purposes of controlled communication the representatives of parties can be persons, official or unofficial, who are in the view of the responsible and representative leaders adequately aware of the attitudes and policies of their governments. A mediator needs to deal directly with decision-makers; it is they and only they who can consider compromises and suggestions, or commit their governments to a course of action. Controlled communication, being a stage prior to negotiation between the parties, being exploratory of relationships, and aiming to reveal underlying causes of conflict, can effectively be conducted at lower decision-making levels – provided, of course, that there is communication with decision-makers as and when required. Indeed, there are some advantages in having around a table officials and even private persons who, as persons, are freer than politicians could be to explore, to examine critically their stereotypes, and generally to stand back from the situation so as to look analytically at the reactions of their political leaders. In discussion experience has been that senior officials sometimes are led to express a government viewpoint, or to explain a reaction, at the same time indicating that they, as persons, are able to see the irrelevant nature of the reaction. Because controlled communication is based upon the assumption that conflict avoidance and resolution are possible by bringing about altered perceptions, by offering different interpretations of behaviour and changed assessments of values and costs, and by drawing attention to options not previously considered, flexibility of participants is essential. Politicians who have personally declared their positions, and whose reactions and perceptions are being analysed, would tend to be rigid and to act defensively.

There are advantages in having around the table persons representing the parties who have sufficient educational background to enable them to participate in the analytical and learning process of discussion. In practice this is generally the case: some academic background is usual. Very soon an atmosphere can be produced, by various means of control later to be described, that enables participants to treat the conflict, not as a contest, but as a problem to be solved.

The ambiguity of the role of representatives – whether they are acting as official representatives in expressing viewpoints, or whether as honorary academics participating in an exercise designed to examine conflict – is itself an asset. It provides a reason for exploration even on matters on which official policy has been firmly stated, it makes possible a working relationship between the participants as persons, and it removes any implications of official commitments. Traditional means of peaceful settlement require commitment: this procedure depends for its success on the absence of any commitment, and the establishment of relationships that do not require it.

This is not to say that representatives are required who are so academic that they are open-minded and easily persuaded. On the contrary, persons are required who tend as persons to be committed to more extreme attitudes. An official or person who does not identify emotionally with the values of the party he represents is not helpful: the underlying issues are not brought to the surface by an apologist, or by a disinterested person. In any event, altered perceptions by such a person would carry little weight with final decision-makers.

The advantage of representatives at the official level is greater at the stage at which functional cooperation is being discussed – a stage reached once communication has effectively been controlled. Politicians are not usually equipped or inclined to discuss details of cooperation, procedures of consultation and alternatives to conflict. They are better equipped, and it is their role, to make judgements on alternatives put forward after they have been worked out in some detail. Functional cooperation between India and Pakistan, or the two communities in Cyprus, or Israel and the Arab States, provides a basis for less hostile behavioural patterns, as it does in international organisation. A good deal of attention is given to functional cooperation in any controlled situation.

The fact that discussion is exploratory, aimed at defining the problem and clarifying attitudes, and is not primarily a negotiation, enables a great deal of flexibility in procedures, and in particular in the selection of representatives. Clearly it would be difficult for formal decision-makers to be in direct communication, even under the United Nations or a mediator, while violence persists. In some circumstances where the parties do not recognise each other, as for example in the Middle East crisis of 1967, it is not even necessary to have nationals representing the parties in initial exploratory talks designed to define the problem. There are nationals of other states who can identify with the belligerents. There can be progressive movements from less to more official representation as exploration reveals some profit in discussion.

There is an important language problem. In discussions of this kind a great deal sometimes hinges upon slightly different uses of words. Two parties that had refused to meet together under any other auspices found that the reasons that had been conveyed through a mediator had been misinterpreted. Conditions had been stated which were interpreted as determining the agenda, whereas in fact they were merely intended to indicate the status of the representatives while they were participating in any discussions. Even though all concerned believe that their English – the language used in this project – is wholly adequate, there are always high probabilities of misunderstandings when English is the second language of the participants. Too much is lost in translation, no matter how good, for effective communication, and representatives need therefore to be selected having the language problem in mind.

(ii) COMMUNICATION BETWEEN REPRESENTATIVES
AND PRINCIPALS

The role of a representative of a party is straightforward
when analysis of conflict is the sole objective of controlled communication. He makes known the viewpoints
of those he represents, even though he may not agree with
them entirely, and even though he may change his own
during communication with the opposing party. When,
however, one of the purposes of the exercise is resolution
of conflict, and furthermore by means that rest heavily
upon reperception of the situation and the motivations of
the opposing party, he has an additional and far more
difficult task. He is required to transmit a revised attitude,
to point out sources of misperception, and evidence of
irrelevant response to persons who have not had his
experience of direct communication. He is open to charges
of being disloyal, or being 'brain-washed', and of adopting
attitudes that cut across accepted national policies and
community consensus. In one case a senior official who
had been faithfully representing the viewpoints of his
government, and who was persuaded that there had been a
complicated process of misinterpretation of events due to
specific and determined causes, was hesitant about sending back his report. The representative at a controlled
communication discussion needs to be in a relationship
with his principals that enables him to transmit alterations
in perceptions, and furthermore, in a relationship that can
lead to the internalisation by his principals of any alterations in perceptions he himself undergoes.

There are several ways in which the transmission of
altered perceptions can be helped. As already indicated,
experience in controlled communication is that it is
necessary to have representatives who are known to identify

with more extreme factions – those who adopt a hard line in relation to the opposing party. It is also important that there should be more than one representative of each party present at all discussions. Numbers are a problem. More than a total of twelve to fifteen participants around the table destroys the intimate exchange among academics and the representatives of the parties, and consequently more than three persons from each party would be too many.

The sending of frequent reports is helpful, but there are dangers in this also. Discussion becomes quite academic at times, as when the situation is modelled, and when other cases of conflict are discussed. Issues are raised which from a theoretical point of view seem relevant, but which the parties believe not to be so. Academics have some discussions that are mainly of interest only to them – which help to create the problem-solving atmosphere. Reporting at this stage would give a false picture of what is taking place, and would probably prejudice decision-makers against the discussions no matter what their outcome. Consequently, a great deal depends upon the understanding of the participants, their discretion in communicating, and therefore in their belief that the discussions might be useful from their point of view.

One problem of transmission that cannot be overcome within this framework is that which arises within administrations that are organised in a highly specialised way. In negotiations with the United States government, for example, it appears necessary to have a large number of representatives, sometimes as many as a hundred, each reporting back to various departments of government. The negotiating 'table' becomes a public meeting in which positions are fixed and representatives are obliged to follow a brief. If this form of negotiation is finally necessary, then preliminary controlled communication between a few representatives of the parties is all the more important. The 1968 Paris discussions between North Vietnam and the United States seemed to support this view. The responsibility for coordination of policies and reassessment of goals in relation to costs is in this way thrown back at an early stage upon administrations in ways that do not interfere with communication with the other party to the dispute. If such coordination fails to take place, that is if there is no effective decision-making process within an administration which enables two or three persons adequately to represent the views of the party, then there can be no effective communication, still less any successful negotiation. The face-to-face and small-group nature of controlled communication in this way serves to direct attention to the importance of decision-making within each party, and to avoid situations of stalemate that arise when each party to a dispute is insufficiently united in its view to enable it to alter its perceptions, goals and assessments of interests.

4 The Establishment of Communication

There is communication in all relationships. In human relationships communication flows usually comprise messages and transactions. However, there is communication even in the absence of messages and transactions, as when a group of one nationality is aware of and has sympathy for another group of the same nationality in different regions with which it has no contact. This is the communication of Jewish peoples, of coloured peoples in respect of commonly experienced prejudices, of religious and ideological groups separated by boundaries and political barriers. There can be, no less, antipathetic communications, such as demonstrations of hostility, which prevent the flow of other messages and transactions, and which thereby influence the behaviour and attitudes of the peoples concerned. There is communication whether it be flows of messages or merely relationships that exist in the absence of actual messages and transactions.

In some relationships there may exist only a potentiality of communication, as when a telephone system exists but has not been used. Communities that have the same values and traditions can exist without any mutual awareness of each other. It is not necessary for a system to be in continuous operation for it to exist, nor is it necessary for transactions ever to have taken place. The structural and functional possibility of transactions, or of antipathetic responses, that exist within a relationship endow it with the systemic attribute of communication.

In this sense there is always communication between states, even if only that communication which is inherent within any system of units of the same set: there is interdependence and mutual influence, sympathy or antagonism between sub-systems, or potentiality of such communication.

Messages and transactions that occur are as likely to be a source of false information as they are to be a source of accurate knowledge. They are not necessarily of a character that promotes harmonious relationships among behavioural systems: communication is a tool of conflict as much as it is a tool of peaceful relationships. It is an integral part of relationships, and no social value can be attached to it as such. Whether communication makes for harmonious or for conflicting relationships depends upon its content and perceptions of its content.

(i) EFFECTIVE COMMUNICATION

The technique of controlled communication derives from the hypothesis that conflict occurs as a result of ineffective communication, and that its resolution, therefore, must involve processes by which communication can be made to be effective. By effective communication is meant the deliberate conveying and accurate receipt and interpretation of what was intended should be conveyed, and the full employment of information as received and stored in the allocation and re-allocation of values, interests and goals.

The assumption underlying the employment of controlled communication is that conflict of interests is a subjective phenomenon which occurs when conditions exist that prevent accurate assessments of costs and values, and consideration of alternative means and goals. This has been argued in the companion study. If conflict were due to aggressiveness or expansionist tendencies of states, and if power relations determined the nature and structure of world society, then the settlement of conflict could come about only by third-party intervention, enforcement of a settlement, or the military defeat of one party by another: each state would endeavour to impose its will on another by negotiating a peace settlement after defeat, or in circumstances that acknowledge defeat. Effective communication would then not be part of the process of ending the conflict (except to see whether one party is ready to agree to terms): it would not take place until one side were victorious. If conflict between states were based upon misperceptions, false calculations of costs, failure to perceive alternative means of attaining goals and such behavioural factors, it would follow that there could be mutual gain in resolving it. Consequently, effective communication would be relevant even during fighting. The two different assumptions, and the correspondingly different means of ending conflict, may be described by reference to industrial conflict. There can be refusal to negotiate until one side returns to work (or lifts the lock-out), the settlement being reached only after defeat by one party. There can also be negotiation while strike (or lock-out) continues, agreement being the basis on which work recommences. In the first instance there tends to be no communication until one side surrenders, and in the other there is communication even during conflict. Clearly conflict resolution, as distinct from settlement, must be based upon agreement prior to cessation of conflict; otherwise there would occur a situation of imposed settlement after one party was defeated. The first step in the study of conflict and of conflict resolution is, therefore, to make communication effective.

Whether communication is effective depends upon several different features of it. Communication is intentional or unintentional, it is designed to convey information accurately or to mislead, it is correctly perceived or misperceived, and even when correctly perceived it is interpreted as intended or misinterpreted. Each one of these features is influenced by the form of communication, for example, whether it is verbal or visual, direct or indirect, and by the circumstances in which it takes place, for example, whether in conditions of fear or of security, of knowledge or of prejudice. The complexity and importance of these problems of communication, until recently virtually ignored in the study of inter-state relations, justify an examination of a hypothesis that conflict and ineffective communication are causally related, and the examination of a face-to-face technique in which in controlled circumstances there can be effective communication, and if necessary, verification of the effectiveness of communication by role reversal and playback methods.

In political relations there are many forms of communication, and some of the most widely employed are among the least effective. When President Nasser of the United Arab Republic took control of the Gulf of Aqaba in 1967 he was communicating something to the Israelis. He was, in effect, saying 'for twenty years we have had to put up with a situation, imposed upon the Arab world by Western states, which has been intolerable nationally. We could not previously alter it, nor discuss the consequences to Arabs affected. The military move now places us in an improved bargaining position. From it we can approach the issue of refugees, the future composition, status and role of Israel in the Middle East, and an overall structure that would be

a step towards freeing the Arab world from foreign influences that have distorted its political and economic
development. We have no quarrel with Jewish people as
such; we are in fact the one people. But we cannot
tolerate the presence of an alien state that has been created
at the expense of Arabs, that has already sought, with
Western support, to expand at their further expense, and
which offers a constant threat to all neighbouring Arab
states.' President Nasser had frequently had to speak also
to the Arab world. His messages to them were verbal,
heard by Israelis, and were couched in terms that implied
that the state of Israel must be eliminated so that the
threat to Arabs would be eliminated. The message conveyed to the Israelis by military action was not interpreted
as an invitation to join in down-to-earth discussions. On
the contrary, the message they received as a result of
military moves was more like the verbal message already
conveyed to the Arab world: the military move was perceived as a first step in carrying out a previously made
verbal threat. They interpreted the military move and the
verbal statements as meaning that President Nasser was
intent upon driving all Jews into the sea. They responded
accordingly with a pre-emptive strike. After the cease-fire
the Israelis tried to communicate something by remaining
in occupation of large areas of neighbouring states, and
also failed to communicate what they were saying and to
obtain the sought-for response. They faced the same
problem that President Nasser had faced. They were
required to make statements for public consumption:
there was a delicate balance of power in the government,
and public opinion was clearly in favour of retaining the
'gains of war'. What the government was trying to convey
to President Nasser and the Arab world by the continued
occupation of territory was, 'we won a military victory by a

pre-emptive strike at a time when you were led to believe that we would not take the initiative. But we are not acting as victors: we know that we have not subjugated, and could not subjugate, all Arab states. We cannot even hold on to the areas we are now occupying: the costs in terms of manpower and resources are too great. Nor can we sustain wars every generation or so. Furthermore, we can no longer rely upon the West any more than any state can rely upon any great power. We are geographically in the Middle East and must become a Middle East country. We also have an interest in trying to make the area secure from foreign intervention. We have a role to play once barriers are down and there can be some functional and industrial cooperation. If we were to withdraw now we would have no bargaining position, and would be back where we were; politically it is impossible. It might be possible to withdraw if it could be accepted in principle that we both want to settle outstanding differences in a way which enables us to be a state within the Middle East. The way is open for a substantial measure of demobilisation, disarmament and cooperation in development once normal relations are created. The alternative is for us both to construct missile bases, and for each to have a deterrent second-strike capacity, which neither of us can afford in the face of more pressing demands for development.' This message was not received by President Nasser and other Arab leaders, or by Arabs generally, because it became confused with verbal messages to Israelis which implied that territory would be retained, and because the retention of territory seemed to confirm to all Arabs the aggressive behaviour which they had suspected. Parties to a dispute and in communication by military actions each believe that they have tried to communicate something positive, and each asserts that the other party is plainly aggressive and not communicating any constructive message. Distrust and perception of aggressive intent are mutual. In this particular case, the misperceptions prevented direct discussion. The behaviour of each side reinforced the stereotypes held by each side of the other, and made discussions less and less possible. In due course other values had to be taken into account on both sides, for example, the need in the United Arab Republic to settle the dispute by some means which enabled Arabs to live down the fact of repeated defeat, and the need in Israel to provide for defences that did not rest upon an agreement with Arabs and foreign guarantees.

The use of power and threat as means of communication is very old; the history of such communication is that it is inefficient and leads to misinformation. The only means of testing to see whether the messages were as received, or were as each side says they were intended, is for some direct communication by verbal and visual means. But parties in conflict usually do not have these means at their disposal, or even feel free to use them when they do; it is for this reason that they use military smoke signals. Direct or indirect verbal communication cannot be used for fear of appearing to be giving in, and for fear of public reactions.

Diplomacy provides direct or indirect verbal communication. However, it is sometimes not far removed from this military form. It takes place within a power framework. It is subject to many of the same misinterpretations. It communicates knowledge, threats and bargains. Misinformation or 'noise' is part of the communication of diplomacy. Intelligence services provide information that is interpreted in the light of established ideologies, theories and stereotypes, and are the source of a great deal of misinformation. Press reports, press conferences and official statements are means of communication, and what is communicated is frequently a distortion of attitude or policy, and is further distorted when interpreted by the receiver. In the power relations of states communication is rarely effective. Furthermore, diplomatic communication is universally within a framework of conventional wisdom that does not invite consideration of policy alternatives and options that are possible. A systems approach to conflict in Nigeria, and to disputes existing between Somalia, Ethiopia and Kenya invites sociological questions of legitimisation and transactions of great political relevance and practical importance to disputes about local jurisdiction and boundaries. No matter how efficient and straightforward diplomatic communication might be, it is limited by the conceptual thinking that prevails. Even the diplomatic perception of relationships is in a restricted framework: decision-makers tend 'to fit incoming information into their existing theories and images'.[1] Communication is effective only when there is a check on and flexibility in processes of perception and of consideration of responses.

Since the resolution of conflict depends upon effective communication, it can come only from the parties themselves. Processes are required that alter perceptions, and promote the points of view of the parties, and not of third parties. The process of resolution of conflict is essentially the process of testing whether information is received as was transmitted, and whether what was transmitted was sent deliberately and contained accurate information. Effective communication and its testing are difficult enough even among states that are in harmonious relationships and have the advantages of diplomatic relations, and ordinary commercial and other transactions. It is all the more difficult in a conflict situation. Indeed, the predisposition of states engaged in conflict to misperceive renders these ordinary means of communication ineffective, and nothing short of face-to-face discussion within a controlled framework is likely to be adequate. The differences between societies and communities are differences in levels and in purposes of communication: in the former it is a means of peaceful coexistence, and in the latter it is a value in itself. Controlled communication between parties in dispute is an attempt to raise the level of communication to transform competitive and conflicting relationships into ones in which common values are being sought. For this to happen hitherto unexplored alternatives suggested by untraditional models and concepts, need to be introduced into discussions.

(ii) THE ESTABLISHMENT OF EFFECTIVE COMMUNICATION

The establishment between parties to a dispute of communication of a character that can test the accuracy of information received presents problems of its own. Initiatives by one party are inhibited by fear that they will be perceived as a confession of weakness or of defeat. Even when taken they may be perceived as a trick. If made public they might lessen the resolve of those engaged in conflict. Furthermore, a willingness to negotiate might imply a willingness to compromise, and leaders of parties to a dispute are rarely in a position to demonstrate such a willingness. There are sometimes procedural means of overcoming some of these difficulties, including third-party initiatives, and informal and secret communication between parties. It is noteworthy that even states in conflict maintain some communication, for example, the United States of America and the Peoples' Republic of

China have some direct exchanges through diplomatic representatives. However, communication of this type could readily reinforce attitudes, and increase tensions.

In the project with which we are dealing, parties in violent conflict were invited to assist in a research programme. As discussions were to be in secret, there were no serious political problems involved. Even if the fact of discussions were to have become known no great damage could be done since governments were merely cooperating in an academic exercise. No party was implying that it desired to resolve the conflict, that it thought a solution was possible, that it was prepared even to contemplate altering its position, or that those participating were in any position to do more than to interpret government policies and attitudes that had already been made public. On the contrary, acceptance of invitations was usually accompanied by assertions that negotiations of any kind to arrive at a solution of the problem were a waste of time because of the dishonesty and aggressive designs of the other party.

A decision by a party engaged in an on-going dispute, especially one in which violence is taking place, to enter into discussions even in an academic framework with the opposing party or parties that may not even be 'recognised', is one which can be taken only by the head of government, or the leader of the community involved. For this reason invitations or requests to participate were directed to the head of government or the responsible minister. Messages sent through administrations, for example overseas missions, produce negative results, and the reason seems to be that it is easier to say no to an unusual request which requires a decision at a high level than to obtain consideration at that level. Administrations are not good at handling unusual situations. Whenever direct contact could be made with decision-makers the unusualness of the request was in some respects an asset: it was a challenge to decision-making and evoked interested responses.

A short document cannot explain the technique and answer the many questions that are raised, and a long one is not read. Consequently it was found necessary to follow up a letter with a personal visit to the decision-maker concerned. Responses at this level were usually positive even though discussions were not finally arranged in all cases. Criticism of traditional methods, the need for informal approaches, an interest in comparative conflict studies, suspicion of great powers, and of the United Nations which is dominated by them, were general, as were questions about the sources of funds for the research project, and the motivations of those engaged in it. The country, the university in the country, and the persons involved were all relevant considerations in some cases. An impression was obtained that decision-makers welcomed an academic interest in the complex problems of conflict, but were highly suspicious of motivations and sponsors.

Because controlled communication is somewhat novel as a technique, yet sufficiently closely related to traditional methods to be confused with them, its nature needs to be understood by the parties before they make decisions about participation. Indeed, one reason for this report at this early stage of the project is to provide a detailed exposition which fully explains what is being put forward, and which can supplement verbal explanations.

In passing it is relevant to observe that comparative studies and insights into decision-making processes are assisted as a result of the type of field work required in preparation. Information flows, information blockage, overloading, the role and influence of the individual, the boundaries of thought and awareness of officials and ministers, the gap between the level of knowledge available and the level of knowledge within the decision-making bodies, prejudice, stereotypes and mirror images are all on display. Anyone who has worked within a foreign office knows something of these phenomena, but little on a comparative basis. Opportunity was taken of these visits to obtain an impression of some of the essential features of the conflict. It will be noted later when discussing the role of third parties in this framework that knowledge of the situation may be a liability; but in order to prepare relevant propositions and models of the situation, and to draw attention to theories and past empirical work that might be related, it is necessary to know in advance whether there are internal conflicts within the parties themselves, something of the ethnic and other divisions, interdependence relationships with other states, and other such features that are not always obvious in ordinary reporting. Propositions and questions can then be drafted and discussed in advance by the panel, thereby ensuring that the greatest possible use is made of the opportunities afforded by these discussions.

NOTE TO CHAPTER FOUR

(1) See Jervis, 'Hypotheses of Misperception', for an important contribution on hypotheses of misperception.

5 The Control of Communication

Before turning to procedures and tactics of control, some comment needs to be made on the role of third parties, in this case a panel of political and social scientists. A good deal has been written on this subject. Most has been in connection with traditional means of peaceful settlement. The role of the third party in these circumstances ranges from intervention to enforce an agreement, to an exercise of whatever influence is possible by bringing reason to bear upon the problem.

Young has described the role of third parties in terms that would be generally acceptable to most political scientists, and indeed, to most contemporary mediators.

> The role of the third party may, however, vary substantially along such axes as the following: formality-informality, extensiveness of the resources committed by the third party, directness of penetration into the two-sided bargaining processes, and identity of the intervening party. But the role is ultimately directed towards aiding the parties to a crisis to realise their own common or overlapping interests when various problems threaten to disrupt or severely downgrade their bargaining relationship. In this sense the third party attempts to help both sides rather than to tip the

balance towards one or the other. Finally, it should be noted explicitly that there is a real difference between regulating and terminating a crisis on the one hand and reaching a substantive settlement of the underlying issues. Especially in international conflicts, it may be possible to reach a real settlement only over an extended period of time. But third-party intervention may, nevertheless, be of great importance in terminating a given crisis in the sense of reducing the threat of violence in the system and bringing the destabilizing impact of the crisis under control.[1]

He then goes on to explain the way in which even the presence of a third party alters the behaviour of the disputing parties. Misunderstandings can be cleared up by a third party, the disputing parties are more inclined to listen to each other, emotional levels can be reduced, the power relations of the parties can be balanced so that solutions reflect basic issues and not these relations, and alternative viewpoints can be put forward in ways that allow the parties to move away from stances that have been adopted. These are all important functions of the third party in any mediation role, be it industrial or international. Young outlines functions that are particularly relevant to international mediation, including data collection and processing, and verification of statements.[2] This is a valuable exposition of functions and tactics required in the traditional role of a mediator.

The role of the third party in controlled communication is a different one. In one sense it is less active: it is not to persuade, and probably not to verify or to be a judge of the accuracy of statements made, or a judge of the reasonableness of argument. In another sense it is far more active, and this is the distinctive difference. The third party in controlled communication is there to explain conflict, its origins, its escalation, sometimes by reference to other conflicts, sometimes by analytical means, but within the context of a continuing discussion between the parties.

The main differences in function of the third party arise out of the difference in objective. Traditional mediation seeks agreements by compromises, or by persuading the parties that their best interests would be served by ceasing violence and arriving at a settlement. It is a negotiating framework. Controlled communication, on the other hand, endeavours to establish a condition in which the parties see their relationships as posing a problem to be solved. Both sides are assumed to have been acting in ways which appear to them, in the light of the knowledge they have, and the circumstances in which they operate, to be in their best interests. Neither is more right nor wrong than the other. Even if an aggressive initiative has been wholly with one side, even if there appears to have been a blatant case of unprovoked aggression, there is still a problem: the apparent aggression was stimulated by some circumstances, and it is in the interest of the suffering party to help solve the problem. The role of the third party is to establish a condition in which all the parties join with it in defining, identifying and solving the problem.

Experience has shown that one of the qualifications required in the third party is an ignorance of the situation, and if necessary a simulated ignorance. Any panel member who has studied the situation under discussion, or has committed himself to any view of it, is unsuitable as a panel member. He listens with an ear tuned to conclusions he has already arrived at. The parties must state the problem as they see it, and exchange views about it to clarify it, promoted by questions from the panel which at times may seem naïve and based on ignorance of most elemental features. Gradually confidence is built up in the panel when it is seen that questions have a point, and lead to clarifications, and as the relevance of comparative situations becomes clearer.

This is not just a pose or a tactic. No matter how close a study one may have made of a particular conflict, it appears quite different once it is expounded by the parties and after they have cross-examined each other. There are psychological reasons why resolution of a conflict must come from the parties themselves, and not be suggested by third parties; but there are also reasons of analysis. It is only the parties that can point to the relevant issues as they perceive them: the conflict is at least in part a perceived relationship, and only the parties can describe and explain some aspects of it.

Panel members are political and social scientists who have worked in the fields of conflict, including the related areas of decision-making, perception, deterrence, escalation, functionalism, and the very many other aspects that are now the subject of empirical research. Experienced diplomats, journalists, historians and others who do not have this type of academic background can make little contribution: the role of the third party is to make available a body of knowledge on which the parties can draw, and it is a specialised knowledge that they would not normally have. They already have whatever can be supplied by practitioners and students of traditional studies. Having in mind that it is only a small proportion of persons who are sufficiently sensitive to take part in delicate discussions such as take place, and having in mind the few scholars working in this area, it is not surprising that it is not easy to find suitable panels without drawing upon the resources of several countries. There should be no problem in the years to come as more and more students are now receiving an appropriate training, and practical experience in role reversing and perception.

It needs to be emphasised, however, that it is no more the role of the third party to impose theoretical explanations than it is to suggest practical solutions. A body of theory is in the minds of the panel, relevant questions are asked as a result. Some are quickly found not to be relevant, others seem to be dodged and may be pressed, but any political scientist who is committed to a theoretical explanation or solution is as disruptive around the table as the regional expert who has made his own study of the particular conflict. The parties must select what is relevant, the panel merely making a general first selection from a vast body of theoretical and comparative studies to short cut what would otherwise be an impossible task for the parties.

The ability of the members of the panel to identify with both parties is an essential one. This is difficult for some scholars who have various normative notions of behaviour, and who are inclined to regard behaviour as being right or wrong in some sense. Experience is that lawyers make poor panel members. So do rigid pacifists, or others whose value systems lead them to make judgements of behaviour. For political scientists who base their thinking upon systems behaviour, and systems response to the environment, it is not difficult to identify with all parties to a dispute, and to accept that each acted in good faith in responding to circumstances in ways thought at the time to be relevant. That the parties were misled by lack of knowledge, by perceptions that were subsequently shown to be false, by prejudice or cultural limitations, is acknowledged without this in any way reflecting upon the perceived relevance of the behaviour at the time it took place.

There are persons who seem to be more sensitive than others and know when to intervene, when to press a point and when not to do so, and as with all mediation this factor is of the greatest importance in the selection of panel members in controlled communication. This applies to relationships at informal gatherings as much as when round the table: in practice coffee breaks are a continuation of discussions. Suspicions are never wholly eliminated, and the representative of one party very quickly detects personal friendships growing between panel members and the representatives of the other party.

(ii) PREPARATION

It has been found useful to conduct a seminar before a session with the academic panel and other scholars who might be interested. Propositions are then formulated that might appear at first sight to be relevant to the situation, comparative situations are discussed, and the main questions that need to be asked are listed. This is helpful in making sure that the greatest possible advantage is taken of the situation in order to put propositions to a test, but it is also useful from the point of view of resolution of conflict because it helps panel members to focus upon those aspects of contemporary theory that are likely to be most relevant. For example, while all disputes have behavioural features in common, some special aspects of theory are relevant to a border dispute, a communal conflict, a social or political revolution or a third-party intervention in support of an unpopular government. The effectiveness of controlled communication rests upon the degree to which the panel can bring to bear relevant knowledge, and preparation along these lines is essential. However, the situation once described by the parties presents facets not previously considered, and these panel discussions seem to be necessary after each day's meeting in preparation for the next. A seminar after meetings have concluded, again with other academics, gives an opportunity to assess the degree to which expectations were fulfilled, the way in which propositions had to be restated, and the features that emerged which seem to throw light upon conflict generally, and the techniques of handling it.

(iii) PRELIMINARY ARRANGEMENTS

Understandably, when the representatives of parties that are in violent conflict meet for a first time there is an atmosphere of acute tension. There is tension at meetings of the Security Council when parties are present together and attack each other in public. In the informal atmosphere of controlled communication the tension is at a more intimate level. The parties have agreed to sit together, and not for purposes of scoring bargaining points, but to analyse a problem. They are in the same room, but there is no contact, and they talk separately with panel members. It is not unusual for the representatives to know each other, to have worked with each other in the past, as when a state has been partitioned, or when two states have been in close contact prior to conflict. In any event, the diplomatic community in world society is a small one and movements are frequent among them. If representatives know each other a degree of rationalisation is possible: each takes a sympathetic view of the other who, as a person, is unfortunately involved in policies for which he could not possibly be responsible and which he would not personally support. However, the tension remains even in these circumstances, made all the higher, perhaps, because panel members are aware of it, and on the watch for signs of it.

Seating round the table is not an unimportant detail. The party to the left of the chairman is seen as being discriminated against, and if there is a 'legal' and a 'rebel' party, the latter can be most sensitive to such placing. Both parties must be in a position to focus on the chairman or on active panel members to avoid the embarrassment, in the early stages, of talking across the table to the opposition. Yet both parties must be in a position to talk directly when they feel free to do so. On one occasion a T-shaped table created unforeseen difficulties, and the parties did not communicate until advantage was taken of the temporary absence of a participant to alter seating. A long oblong one was tried on one occasion, and this provided a sufficient structure to enable a focus on the chairman, and at the same time to allow interaction across the table between the parties. Depending upon the degree of informality that can be introduced from the beginning, a round table is probably ideal, but sufficiently large ones are not often available. An informal circle around a low table is an alternative, but this tends to detract from the seriousness of the academic framework in which people need to be taking notes, and moreover, there is a need for the formality of a table separating speakers. Whatever the initial arrangements, random alterations in seating arranged on the basis of first come first served have some advantages after the first few sessions. The only person who needs to maintain the one position is the chairman who provides the focal point about which others arrange themselves. The role of chairman is to provide this focal point, but very little more outside calling for the tea breaks. The conduct and control of discussion is by the interventions of members of the academic panel. In due course what emerges is a highly sophisticated seminar discussion as might take place among experienced staff members of an interdisciplinary university department.

There is no agenda. The purpose of the discourse is

clear in the invitation, and is further clarified by introductory remarks. The parties are invited at an early stage
to describe the conflict as they see it, wholly uninhibited
by diplomatic or any other conventions, as is possible in an
academic framework. Official presentations of the case
follow, with accusations and counter-accusations. Very
little of this provides new information; but an official
obligation is being fulfilled. After these expositions are
complete, which usually takes at least one day, questions
are asked by panel members and by the parties.

(iv) THE CONTROL OF COMMUNICATION

Following this opening the first steps are taken to control
the discussion. It needs to be appreciated that the parties
come conditioned in their behaviour by all the communication, intended and unintended, misleading and accurate,
correctly and falsely received and interpreted, as outlined
in the previous chapter.

The strategies of control seem to be those of the clinical
psychoanalyst, the caseworker, the industrial psychologist
and the family counsellor. They take for granted the
existence of stereotypes and entrenched positions. The
analyst and the social caseworker are concerned with
problems faced by the individual, and attempt to assist an
inadequate person dealing with an over-oppressive environment. The client is most usually maladjusted in some way.
It might seem a far cry from casework to resolution of
conflict between states; states are not maladjusted individuals, and the representatives of states are invariably
intelligent, aware and highly informed persons. Yet, the
experience of casework, and the 'supportive' approach of
the caseworker, are most relevant; caseworkers have had
to face the problems involved when identification with a

party is essential, when approval is necessary of actions within the context of their enactment, while still maintaining the objectivity that is needed in order to ask the appropriate question or to make the leading comment. The social and international analysts require many of the same techniques: the techniques used for lessening tension in the interviewee; for bringing or keeping the interviewee to the main issue; for helping the interviewee to make difficult admissions; for breaking defence mechanisms; for influencing the judgement of the interviewee; to help the interviewer to gain time; to help the interviewer to recover from a bad start.[3] Clarifications, the promotion of insights into the position of each party by the other, correction of perceptions, explanation of international processes of interaction, all require the techniques, skills and experience of the caseworker. Psychoanalysis, psychotherapy, group therapy and resolution of conflict between parties to disputes all have much in common; they all involve professional relationships, and invite the same kinds of professional behavioural patterns. The technique establishes a discourse, not merely between parties and the third party. The third party provides a reference framework, not someone to whom an appeal can be made on historical, legal or moral grounds, but someone able to demonstrate features that commonly occur, thus allowing parties to view their problem, not as a unique and insoluble one, but as one that has features which are usual. Behaviour is then perceived as a common response to environmental circumstances.

It is important that the third party resists invitations to become a judge. Parties in dispute appeal to history, to law, to conscience and to humanitarian values.[4] They enter into discussions prepared to appeal on these grounds to the analysts present. To control this it is useful to demonstrate at the outset that contemporary social science has moved away from the normative approaches of religion and law, in which behaviour is designated as right or wrong, legal or illegal, just or unjust, defensive or aggressive, according to canons already determined; analysis of conflict is analysis of behavioural responses to circumstances, of possible alternative responses, of possible false perceptions, and the behaviour of the parties is not being judged at any stage. The use of normative terms, and reference to normative values, have only a propaganda function; if allowed in analytical discussions they decrease communication, and cloud analysis.

Parties also come with a view to making a case for some particular solution, and they believe that if their appeals succeed, then their solutions will find acceptance. Parties to conflict are so accustomed, because of traditional diplomatic and power practices, to a negotiating framework, that they act on the assumption that in their discussions, one side will gain and another will lose. To control this it is useful to stress that analysis is not concerned with examining the merits of alternative solutions. A resolution of conflict may be suggested as the result of analysis; but it is far more likely that altered perceptions and attitudes will lead to solutions quite different from those contemplated by any party. The exercise is not a contest. On the contrary, controlled communication is based on quite different assumptions. It is not assumed that conflict is like an economic struggle for scarce resources, in which gain by one implies loss by another; it assumes that analysis will reveal, after perceptions are corrected, that neither side may be required to compromise, and that solutions will be found by which all gain. These two features, the absence of normative and of bargaining attitudes, can best be demonstrated by showing directions in which social sciences have been moving. For this purpose the diagram on page 223 can be used.

Experience has shown that the problem of control can be made easier by an introductory exposition from a panel member about the nature of controlled communication, and the ways in which social science has developed. These introductory remarks need to be fitted to the occasion: at the opening the situation is a tense one, and too much academic talk at this stage seems to be delaying proceedings and to be irrelevant.

Parties tend to assume that their particular conflict is unique, and less susceptible to analysis and resolution than may be the case with others. Even parties involved in racial conflicts seem to think they are experiencing unprecedented situations. It is useful to refer constantly to other situations that have similar characteristics, for example, long-standing communal problems, traditional antagonisms, colonial histories, and third-party interference. Knowledge that the conflict under discussion is not unique in most of its basic features, that all parties tend to make the same appeals, that escalation takes place, that the opposing party has the same feelings of hostility and injustice, help in making the exercise a problem-solving one rather than a contest.

One unique feature of their conflicts appears to parties to be the intensity of fear and antagonism. Especially at the early stages of analysis, parties are eager to put their case, and to dwell upon the atrocities of others. This can be controlled by demonstrating that all parties are guilty of behaviour that is indefensible on moral and humanitarian grounds, and that the reason is the escalation of conflict that takes place once tension occurs. An explanation of escalation helps parties to justify to themselves their own excesses, and to see the degree to which escalation is merely the weighty superstructure built upon a perception of minor threats. A simple drawing can show the processes by which conflict escalates from an initial action by one party, which is perceived by another party as a threat, and reacted to in a manner calling forth a further reaction from the initiator. Intensity of response spirals through further actions and reactions, commencing with diplomatic notes, proceeding through economic pressure and troop mobilisation, and ending with war. It can be explained that an action is usually perceived by the other party as being far stronger than intended by its initiator, and that the hostile reaction of the other party is interpreted as confirmation of the hypothesis that led to a preceding action.[5]

The specific strategies of control that achieve their purpose are those calculated to promote abstract discussion of the concrete situation. Abstract models help parties to observe the basis of conflict, and in particular to discern the processes and effects of escalation. Their own accusations and counter-accusations about atrocities and provocations come to be perceived within this framework of behavioural responses and escalation processes, thus making possible a less subjective interpretation of events. Once the past is reperceived and the violence explained, the future can be considered within a less fearful framework. The effect on the parties of an awareness of the processes of perception is a striking feature of this controlled communication. In short, the parties are helped not by the third party as such, but by the ordinary academic tools of analysis, to stand back from their conflict, and to understand its origins and its manifestations. Once each party is in a position to perceive the problem from a behavioural point of view of the other, communication is effectively controlled, and tends to become constructive.

(v) PERCEPTION

The main means of control relate to an understanding of perception and to the making of true and false inferences. The exercise is one primarily of what may be called 'reperception', and there can be no reperception in the absence of a realisation that different perceptions are possible. It is not appropriate to give lectures to participants about perceptions as though they were students, but control does depend to a significant degree upon an understanding by the participants of the reasons for their attitudes and responses, and upon a realisation that there is the possibility of false perception. According to the circumstances, some demonstration of visual perceptions is usually possible, in passing as it were, and from this observations can be made about non-visual perception. The figures below taken from various sources are examples.[6]

Parties to a conflict have most rigid ideas about the character and motives of their opponents. They have usually experienced many years of conflict and their selections from past history and their moral judgements justify, confirm and reinforce their attitudes. To a third party their images of their opponents appear distorted; no man could so consistently be irrational, immoral and untrustworthy as one party is perceived to be by the other. That there is distortion is even clearer when it is discovered that each party has the same favourable image of itself and its behaviour, and the same unfavourable and treacherous one of the other. The initial problem is to demonstrate that these mirror images exist, that each party is making identical accusations about the other on the same kind of evidence. If the third party argues the case of one party, or in any way tries to demonstrate that an image or an interpretation of events is false, he prejudices his relationships with that party. Both sides must find out for themselves that their perceptions and interpretations may be false.

Demonstrations of the possibility of false visual perceptions help to make the point, without in any way requiring the third party to enter into the debate. For example, Figures 1 and 2 show how it is possible to perceive and to have a mental image of things that cannot in fact exist. It is only when one examines carefully the details, and relates these to experience that the reasons why they cannot exist become clear. The stereotypes that East and West have had of each other are of this kind; analytical attention to detail would probably alter attitudes. Figure 3 shows, on the other hand, how it is possible not to have any clear image of something that does exist, at least until some patterns have been observed through careful examination. At first sight the patches are meaningless. Eventually a pattern that is meaningful is observed, and once this has emerged it is difficult not to see this pattern. (The key is to be found in Figure 10.)

It is also useful to show that more than one image can be seen in the one set of relationships. Figure 4 may be interpreted as a very old lady or as a young girl. One set of political events and behavioural patterns can be interpreted as aggressive, or in some other way, according to the processes of perception that take place within the observer. In this case the observer can flash from one interpretation to another. What needs to be demonstrated is that all observation is preconditioned by experience – and by prejudice. Most people can make no sense of the policies, attitudes and responses of a foreign state, but once knowledge is available patterns emerge. Something of this nature occurred in Soviet–United States relations in the sixties.

This cannot easily be argued in a controlled communication context as a psychologist or neurologist might seek

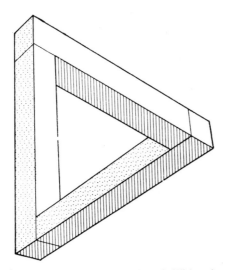

FIG. 1. An 'impossible object'. This triangle cannot exist. [From L. S. Penrose
and R. Penrose, in *British Journal of Psychology*, vol. 49 (1958) p. 31.]

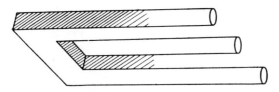

FIG. 2. The trouble with all these objects is over
the third dimension. The perceptual system has
to construct three dimensions from the two given by
the image at the eye; here the information is contradictory, and it fails.

FIG. 2. The Hidden Man. [After P. B. Porter, in *American Journal of Psychology* (1954) p. 552.]

FIG. 4. Which is it—an old woman with chin sunk in wrap, or the heroine of an early twentieth-century romantic novel, her chin in air?

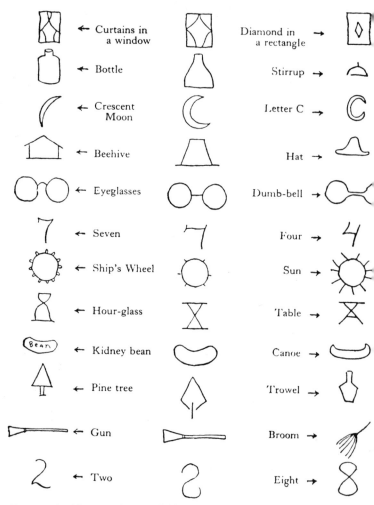

FIG. 5. Ambiguous figures (*After* L. Carmichael *et al.* in *Journal of Experimental Psychology*, vol. 15, p. 80.)

PARIS IN THE THE SPRING

ONCE IN A A LIFETIME

BIRD IN THE THE HAND

Fɪɢ. 6. The Three Triangles. (Read the statement in each triangle.) (*After* R. Brooks)

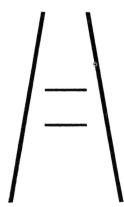

Fɪɢ. 7. The Ponzo illusion. This also is famous: the upper of the two horizontals appears the longer. The distortion is produced by the converging lines.

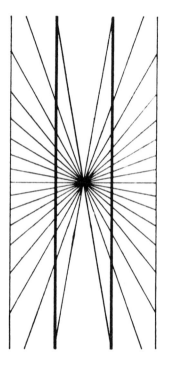

Fig. 8. The Hering illusion. This striking bending of the verticals is produced by the radiating background lines. (These illusions also occur when they are rotated, the distortions being in the same direction, within the figure, and roughly to the same extent.)

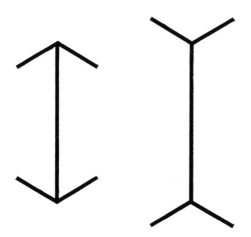

FIG. 9. The Muller-Lyer illusion figure. One of the most famous of the distortion-illusions: it is *itself* distorted, while most of the distortions are *produced* on some lines by others.

to do.[7] It can be suggested by reporting an experiment once conducted in which two groups were asked to draw what they had seen, one being given one set of titles to a series of objects, and one another. What was drawn by each group was different and tended to be more like the objects indicated by the title than the objects that had been seen, as Figure 5 shows.

The strong tendency for the observer not to see detail can be shown by glancing at and then re-examining Figure 6. The effect upon observation of environmental factors can be demonstrated by Figures 7, 8 and 9.

In these ways parties to a conflict can be persuaded that the assumptions they make about the behaviour of others are a consequence of their experiences, which are based upon perceptions, which themselves are conditioned by their attitudes and expectations in the environment in which they are observing and making judgements. The processes that lead to reinforcement and certainty can by these means be explained, at least sufficiently to suggest that all evidence must be tested by some means to ensure that it is being correctly interpreted.

The relationship between visual and non-visual images cannot readily be demonstrated: there is probably little more than useful analogy present. However, consideration of visual misperception paves the way for meaningful discussion. It is possible in these ways to build up a situation in which parties are able to tolerate 'the expression of hostility in a relationship in which it is customarily suppressed',[8] which is an important feature of effective communication between parties in conflict.

(vi) THE MODELLING OF CONFLICT

Control of conflict can usually be established by these means within eight or ten hours of discussion – soon after parties have had the opportunity to state their positions and to question each other. Once established it can be maintained by introducing gradually appropriate models of the conflict being discussed. Some examples are included in the companion study where they were relevant to discussion of conflict. These do not mean much at first glance, but it must be remembered that they are built up spontaneously as part of the discussion, and line by line in front of the parties. The building of models, and the reasons for their details are part of an exposition of a notion or a theory, and completed models become a shorthand method of describing complex ideas; they become part of the language subsequently used in communication.

It will at once be clear that the models, especially when produced by the panel, are suggesting explanations and leading to possible solutions. For example, a model of a communal conflict[9] might suggest the need for a federal structure in which one legislature provides the common needs, and separate legislatures the ethnic needs of a multi-ethnic community. There are dangers in this: the panel can easily slip into the role of mediator or conciliator, making suggestions that should be coming from the parties. The model building needs to develop out of the discussion, and not be just an opportunity for scholars to introduce their favourite schemes. At the same time, one of the roles of the third party is to inject new ideas into the total situation so that discussion is more than negotiation with no input except that which comes from parties. A balance is struck by putting forward models that are suggested by discussion, but not pressing them upon the discussion if they are not taken up by the parties.

This discussion of models is an appropriate place at which to draw attention to the failure of a good deal of traditional mediation because of the existence in the background of conventionalised views and models that have little relevance to contemporary world society. Two examples will demonstrate this, one where resolution appeared to be possible as the result of a break from traditional approaches, and one where fighting followed an attempt to apply a traditional model.

The Kenya–Somalia dispute raised difficult problems of boundaries, minority populations and movements of non-nationals across boundaries. In traditional terms this was a boundary dispute, and the solution was boundary change, perhaps as the result of war, to correct a position inherited by the parties concerned. Legal and historical arguments could have been used by each side with equal effectiveness and were used in a publication by one party. Conflict could have continued to escalate as each side continued the argument and took whatever steps seemed to be necessary to assert its rights. This is one model. Another model of the same situation, and the one that seems to have been used, is a sociological one which gives prominence to transactions across the boundaries, the social realities of the situation, the points at which influence from the opposing parties ceased, leaving the sensitive boundary and sovereignty issues out of the discussion. What then has to be determined is, how are transactions on the ground to be organised so that they will not be disturbed, so that the interests of the sovereign parties will be preserved, so that economic development can be promoted, and other matters of this kind. The issue, according to this model, is not a boundary one, but one of social organisation and functional cooperation between the two parties in respect of the local populations involved.

The Nigerian case of 1967 was one in which traditional notions prevailed, and led to conflict. Here was a case in which certain ethnic groups wished to be responsible for decision-making that affected them, either as a separate state or a separate unit within a wider political organisation. The response of the central government was that it was the legal authority, and that it had a right and a duty to impose law and order. This was also the view generally of other states that indicated an interest in the dispute. This reflected the traditional notion that the *status quo* has some special value and should be maintained, and that what is legal is also legitimised. In the contemporary world society the notion of legality is giving place to the sociological notion of legitimisation, and clearly the legal government had no legitimised status, otherwise there would not have been any break-away movement in the first place. To justify the traditional approach arguments were introduced about the size and viability of states – despite the existence of many smaller African states. An alternative model might have been a model of relationships between separate state organisations, with provisions for functional cooperation to ensure the continuity of existing links which both parties wished to maintain. The traditional model failed to recognise the persistent trends in world society towards greater participation in decision-making, and the creation of smaller units. Separate parliaments for Scotland and Wales would not mean the breaking up of the United Kingdom; they could lead to more direct, and perhaps more efficient, decision-making on matters of local concern. The reason for this reluctance to see smaller administrative units is ironically the belief that a smaller and not a larger number of states is desirable in world society, apparently on the grounds that ultimately a few states might be able to come together in some form of one world. It is apparently thought that boundaries would become less important the fewer the states. But the opposite is the position. Communications and the developments of transactions have made world society a complex of systems that cut across state boundaries, and the role of the state has changed in the process. The small city state was a defensive organisation, even isolationist. The modern world state has the role of facilitating transactions across boundaries, it makes boundaries less relevant, and the more decision-making units there are, the less and not the more significant will boundaries be.[10] It is difficult to justify the use of the traditional model in the case of Nigeria, and the alternative model required at least to be examined so as to determine whether the conflict was to protect the interests of those who happened to be the 'legal' government, or whether there were some wider considerations to be taken into account.

NOTES TO CHAPTER FIVE

(1) Young, *The Intermediaries*, p. 35. See also Meyer, 'Functions of the Mediator in Collective Bargaining', p. 161.
(2) Ibid., pp. 49–79.
(3) See Brown, 'A Review of Casework Methods'.
(4) See North *et al.*, *Content Analysis*.
(5) Ibid.
(6) See, in particular, Abercrombie, *The Anatomy of Judgement;* Foss, *New Horizons in Psychology;* and Thyne, *The Psychology of Learning and Techniques of Teaching*.
(7) Abercrombie, ibid. p. 53.
(8) Ibid. p. 16.
(9) See companion study, p. 48.
(10) Ibid. pp. 28ff.

6 Functionalism and Regionalism

Once control is effective, and once models have been developed which explain important aspects of the conflict to the mutual satisfaction of the parties, the tendency is for discussion to move towards exploration of possible solutions. A first step in this connection is consideration of areas of functional cooperation.

(i) FUNCTIONAL COOPERATION

Consideration of functional cooperation occurs in three different contexts. First, there are the areas of investigation relevant to the analysis of the conflict which require cooperation between the parties, perhaps still with the assistance of the third party. For example, in a communal conflict it is necessary to determine the extent to which tension and conflict exist at the ground level: whether, in fact, there are communal problems in addition to those reflected in leadership and in policies, and which require control or separation of the communities, or whether there are a basic harmony and a common interest that have been destroyed by some temporary interventions such as the policies of colonial powers or prejudices that can be traced to specific sources and instances. Such investigations carried out by the third party have the negative effect of creating tensions between the parties and the third party, as with fact-finding by a conciliator. In practice, functional cooperation in analysing a dispute has limited scope because by the time parties are willing to cooperate they are more interested in steps to resolve conflict and to prevent its reoccurrence than in an examination of the past, even though this would guide them in taking these steps.

Second, there are functional activities that are required to prevent conflict reoccurring. These inevitably relate to suspected causes of conflict. For example, in a communal dispute it is necessary to determine the critical levels of minorities, and where such minorities exist. It seems that very small minorities may not be a source of conflict, while very large ones may enable coexistence in favourable circumstances, as in Malaysia and Fiji. The levels between about fifteen and forty per cent may be critical. (The Report of the Royal Commission on Bilingualism and Biculturalism in Canada in 1967 recommended that both French and English be official languages wherever the minority is more than ten per cent.) Where there are mixed communities there are usually villages and towns where minorities are within the critical range, even though the overall average is not: conflict could commence in these, and by creating unfavourable conditions could upset the precarious stability existing elsewhere. By cooperation in research a source of conflict can be determined and located. Another aspect of the same problem is the connection between ethnic conflict and poverty. There is some evidence that racial conflict is more a function of poverty than of ethnic differences, and is not unlike class conflict within a mono-ethnic society. In mixed communities there are skilled crafts and unskilled occupations traditionally associated with racial groups. Functional cooperation to define this problem, and to see to what extent it can be eliminated by the spread of technical training, is inevitably suggested once the problem is mentioned within the context of controlled communication. The effect upon relations between communities and states of history as taught in schools, and other social matters of this kind, crop up in discussion, and suggest avenues of enquiry on a cooperative basis. It is part of the theory of functionalism that working together on projects assists the processes of cooperation. However, these are typical of the areas of investigation by field work which are suggested by case studies, and which are required for theoretical purposes even though parties are not themselves prepared to carry them out. A research programme in international politics is not complete without field work when it is found that available data are inadequate in relation to hypotheses being investigated.

The third context in which functional cooperation is considered is in the defining of common aims, the finding of alternative means of achieving existing objectives and evolving institutional means of cooperation. Indonesia and Malaysia had to some extent a common interest in confrontation arising out of their own ethnic and political problems. Trading and cultural activities, and regional and defence agreements could possibly produce the same results, especially if deliberately promoted to focus public attention upon economic and social problems to be solved.

Once states have arrived at a relationship in which they are prepared to consider alternative goals and alternative means of achieving existing ones, the conflict is virtually resolved. The stage is not yet set, however, for the technically difficult and time-consuming process of detailed functional cooperation. It cannot be assumed that the felt needs of the parties, that is the areas in which they themselves would be willing to cooperate, and the programmes they agree to explore, reflect the real needs: international collective security was a felt need after 1918, but may not have been the structure required by political relations. Felt needs are not necessarily the needs of the system. Regional plans, like universal collective security institutions, can be thought about, drafted and even accepted by representatives of states; but it does not follow that they are relevant to the future needs of states. In the condition of euphoria which accompanies a prospect of the end of conflict, states tend to consider idealistic schemes which are more related to the personal and political aspirations of leaders than to the realities of systems, states and world society. At this stage the third party has a special role, and is required to inject information into what would otherwise be direct negotiations in which information was lacking other than that already available to the parties. The third party is required to play a conservative, and even a cynical role, to ensure both political realism and an awareness of the problems yet to be solved. For example, it is at this stage that the danger is greatest of representatives of states losing touch with the electorate and the interests they represent. It may seem reasonable for an official and even a political leader to terminate conflict in favour of functional cooperation that achieves the same goal – for example, internal unity – but other interest groups may have been supporting the conflict for different reasons. Resolution of conflict requires the satisfaction of all politically important values.

To some degree the parties can assist each other in overcoming domestic political problems, and this is functional cooperation at a most difficult level. It is for this reason that a bargaining framework, or an attitude of contest needs to be eliminated in favour of an approach designed to solve a common problem. However, even mutual understanding of the problems faced by each other in having proposals accepted, and deliberate mutual assistance in formulating proposals to this end, do not necessarily achieve a stable relationship or resolution of conflict. A role of leadership and government is to determine a consensus. Once a consensus has been determined political leaders are inclined to convince themselves that what was determined by them as a consensus is the national interest, that is, the common goal for which individuals and systems are striving. In reality there are many different goals, and one interpretation of a consensus may be little more valid than another. Indeed, what one knows as national interests and state goals are merely what one deduces after examining policies: one assumes that because a state pursues certain aims they represent state interests. This is not necessarily so; policies are the outcome of innumerable conflicting and competing interests, values and views that contribute to the total decision-making process. All that can be stated with confidence about national interests is that there are systemic requirements of the state and of sub-systems within it relating to continuity of transactions, growth and expectations, adjustment to existing conditions and participation in decision-making – in other words, procedures and processes for unspecified functional purposes, rather than specific goals. It is these, and not felt needs or political objectives, which must control the areas and schemes to be included in functional cooperation. These considerations apply particularly to proposals for regional and wider cooperation in international institutions which, on the surface, seem desirable but which in practice involve states in accepting in the future the decisions of other states on matters of direct interest to them.

Two examples of the way in which political motivations

can lead to proposals that cut across requirements of the political system, thus promoting future conflict, will underline the role of the third party. A typical political reaction to threatened communal conflict has been to give minorities special protection. In Cyprus, Fiji and Malaysia specific discriminations have been written into constitutions to protect minorities, or to deprive growing majorities of proportional political power. There is some evidence in all three situations of a behavioural reaction which is likely to threaten the interests of those being protected: Chinese in Malaysia appear to resent the discrimination against them, for example in recruitment to public services and in the allocation of scholarships, and to react against Malays in ways which might not have occurred in a condition of non-discrimination, and some Malays are sensitive to the fact that it has been thought necessary to have special protection. What was introduced as a temporary felt need to protect Malays has become a source of resentment, and even greater use of this protective device than was originally contemplated seems to be the reaction. Not enough is known of these behavioural responses in any particular situation, but it could be that constitutional revisions to eliminate discrimination are necessary for the avoidance or resolution of conflict. At least there is sufficient theoretical and empirical evidence to suggest that such solutions should not be agreed until the necessary sociological analysis has been made.

A second example of solutions that cut across the requirements of reality is in relation to foreign support. The governments in states that are faced with movements of social and political change tend to seek foreign assistance. It could be that governments that have an expectation of foreign assistance are less inclined to meet demands upon them, and that conflict is ultimately promoted and not avoided by expectations of foreign intervention. Would a British and United States presence in South East Asia make conflict in Malaysia and the Philippines more or less likely? India is undergoing extensive social and political changes, and the authority of the central government may be declining: would expectations of foreign support promote or hinder the social and political compromises that could legitimise government and avoid conflict? These are typical of the questions an academic panel would ask before proposals were discussed for the guarantee of settlements by foreign states. They are also areas of investigation that require field work for academic reasons only.

Assuming that functional cooperation had been promoted, and that studies had provided answers to basic questions, the conditions would then have been established for negotiation between the parties, either with or without a third party. At this stage negotiation is not bargaining; it is discussion of details and administrative planning because the problem has been identified, and analysed in terms of alternative values or options.

In ideal conditions the parties would have the knowledge possessed by the third party, and therefore would have no need for it. A community relationship would have been established. It is only in these conditions that negotiation is a reliable instrument in international politics, and these conditions rest upon the relevant training of decision-makers and their advisers.

(ii) REGIONAL COOPERATION

Experience in controlled communication is that regional cooperation offers a framework for negotiation of functional cooperation. The study of regionalism has only recently received the attention of scholars[1] and in practice regional cooperation has been concentrated upon the defence objectives of the more powerful states involved within a region. SEATO, NATO and the Warsaw Pact are examples. A regional arrangement designed to resolve and to avoid conflict will be durable only if it meets day-to-day continuing needs of all its members. Its purposes and procedures must reflect their requirements. There can be no coerced or privileged members. Consequently, in its drafting, attention needs to be directed in the first instance to the principles of cooperation involved, rather than to the particular needs of some greater states. The mere modification by bargaining processes, of a framework originally designed to suit the needs of only some members, is unlikely to produce a durable agreement.

By 'regionalism' is meant cooperation, whether or not formally structured, between all states within a defined area (excluding any states outside that area) in all matters of inter-state interest. A regional arrangement, so defined, is inward looking: it is concerned with the interests of the states within the region, and does not seek to prejudice the interests of states not in the region, or in any way to offer a threat to other states. SEATO and such defence pacts cannot be described as regional arrangements: they include states outside the region, and not all within it, and they are outward looking in that they seek to confront states in another or the same region.

The positive advantages of regionalism arise out of racial, religious and communal relationships, and insights into behaviour that outsiders cannot have. Even though these dominate, there are usually common regional interests that are best pursued without the interventions of other states, and without involvement in broader conflicts, such as the 'Cold War' confrontations of more powerful states. There are political advantages in regional planning; for example, it enables states to act together and to determine for themselves the conditions of aid or intervention of other states. Regional organisation has the advantages of decentralised organisations; peoples of states within regional organisations are able to identify with them, feel themselves part of them and their decision-making, whereas universal international organisation is remote. There are economies in research and in coordination of activities, and opportunities for integration of functions, without in any way infringing sovereign rights and responsibilities.

Within a regional framework functional cooperation that has a specific and limited purpose, such as health or communication, can be carried out by professional civil servants without reference back to governments except when political considerations emerge. This type of organisation has its own advantages: it removes from the decision-making processes of states a great amount of detail, and allows decisions to be taken at a technical rather than at a political level; it helps to create a high degree of inter-state cooperation based on the common technical and professional interests of the participants, and this cooperation spills over into other matters; and cultural, ideological and other barriers to peaceful relations tend to be removed by cooperation in functional activities.

A regional arrangement, with its functional agencies, will tend to be concerned first and foremost with cooperation in trade and other everyday relations. Any effective intra-defence arrangements must emerge out of this cooperation. External defence arrangements will depend upon circumstances, but there is a reasonable assumption that a regional arrangement that is harmonious internally will require little defence against external forces: international conflict in the contemporary world is frequently a function of internal conflict. One security aim of a regional arrangement is to ensure no member state handles internal tensions in ways likely to invite external intervention. In this sense all states within a regional arrangement have an interest in the internal affairs of other states, and in particular in assisting in every way the solution of each other's internal social problems.

A regional arrangement should plan to continue to function even during strained relations between states; there are examples of functional organisations being attended by states that have no formal diplomatic relations with each other. Frequently, states that have no formal diplomatic relations maintain contact informally. Regional arrangements and their subsidiary functional organisations should, if well-founded, be able to survive any tensions between members, and contribute to their reduction. It follows that the time to introduce a regional arrangement is not after a conflict is resolved, but while it is in existence, and as part of the procedure of resolution. In fact, an arrangement entered into after conflict is settled is in danger of reflecting the pressures that led to its settlement, thus prejudicing the longer-term interests and status of some of the members.

The formal content of an agreement presents few problems. Preamble, purposes, membership, secretariat, organs, powers, procedures for the settlement of disputes, administrative processes and relations with the United Nations and other regional bodies, are among the main matters to be included. The actual drafting in a particular instance should equally present few problems: once membership is determined, and if it is agreed that the basis of decision-making and participation is one of equality, the details of scope and operation are better determined within the organisation, once established, thus avoiding structural inflexibility. However, an agreed framework helps to make organisations politically acceptable.

The problem, therefore, is to ascertain from states their views on many issues that determine the framework of a particular organisation, and to see to what extent these can be incorporated without cutting across theoretical requirements. One way of doing this is to ask questions, such as:

What states are considered within the geo-political region to be covered by the regional arrangement?

Should any state, not located in the region but claiming regional interests and obligations, be given membership, or any observer status?

Should all voting be by unanimity? by unanimity of those voting? by majority?

Is it agreed that all members, no matter what size or economic strength, should be regarded as equal for purposes of voting and participation?

What functions should be given to the regional organisation, and what specialised agencies would be required? (Trade, regional defence, coordination of foreign policies, joint research and training, shipping, development and aid.)

Should the organisation seek recognition by the UN as a regional arrangement under Chapter 8 of the Charter? (Note the implied obligations both of the organisation and of the Security Council.)

Should the organisation seek to incorporate the regional function of the UN specialised agencies?

Should any limits be imposed upon matters to be discussed?

NOTE TO CHAPTER SIX

(1) See, for example, Russett, *International Regions and the International System* and Yalem, *Regionalism and World Order*.

7 Conflict Avoidance

So far we have been concerned with the use of controlled communication in the analysis and resolution of conflict, and in continuation of this, the promotion of functional cooperation between parties. It is in the context of resolving conflict that the technique is most clearly defined, and in which it can be compared with traditional means of peaceful settlement of disputes.

Conflict avoidance is a far more challenging objective because it involves prediction – prediction of likely conflicts, and prediction of future conditions in which they will take place. It could be argued that conflict avoidance is already an important objective of the day-to-day decision-making of administrations, and of the art of diplomacy generally. It could also be claimed to be one of the longer-term objectives of many international institutions, such as the Economic and Social Council and its associated agencies. It is the ultimate end of research institutions that seek to trace the sources of conflicts and to understand their nature. However, no government, international institution or research organisation has developed techniques designed to anticipate and to avoid particular international conflicts. Traditional means of peaceful settlement of disputes are relevant to particular problems after they have arisen, and to events leading up to them.

It is difficult to envisage any circumstances in which they could be employed to anticipate and to avoid possible future conflicts among states and nations.

Conflict avoidance is of two different kinds. One is in respect of likely or anticipated conflicts – those that reasonably can be anticipated because of some observed changes that will in the future alter local relationships, as when the influence of a great power declines in a particular region. The other is in respect of the maintenance of peaceful relationships among states that are already in a close working relationship and do not anticipate the development of tensions. Controlled communication, with its emphasis upon analysis by parties of their own relationships, upon the perceptions that parties have of each other and alternatives available in adjusting to perceived conditions, is as applicable to the peaceful relationships of states as to relationships among states that are, or are likely to be, in conflict. It can be employed, therefore, not only in conflict resolution and in the avoidance of conflicts that can reasonably be anticipated if no steps are taken to avoid them, but also in the maintenance of peaceful relationships even when no source of conflict is currently suspected. It can have a prophylactic as well as a therapeutic function. As such it lends itself to institutionalised forms of regional and international organisation designed to promote peaceful relations and to deal with conflicts if they should arise.

To a limited degree the informal meetings of the British Commonwealth of Nations were an institution that fulfilled these combined functions. In many respects it was a controlled communication exercise in which tensions between members could be brought to the surface in the presence of other members who in some instances could act as a third party. No agenda, no minutes, no publicity, secret discussions and conditions conducive to free expression of attitudes, opportunities to alter attitudes and perceptions, and the absence of bargaining or negotiation were all features of the Prime Ministers' meetings. They lacked the insights and knowledge now available to specialists in the field of world politics, and increased numbers, less informality and a greater number of issues to be handled in the short time available for meetings have helped to destroy their effectiveness.

Whether employed for conflict resolution or conflict avoidance, controlled communication takes the same basic form. It is the parties that are required to project into the future, to define the problems that might occur, to check perceptions and assumptions, to examine their own internal conditions that could spill over into wider conflict, and finally to examine alternative means by which, through functional cooperation or otherwise, possible conflicts might be avoided. The third party has the role of injecting new information about possible trends in world society, the environment in which states will be responding, the changes that are likely to take place in values within the states concerned because of similar changes taking place elsewhere, changing industrial structures and the way in which these will alter international relations generally, and other relevant environmental conditions. In particular, the third party has the function of bringing to attention domestic problems that governments sometimes find more convenient not to consider, and not to admit exist.

The role of the third party in conflict avoidance is more active than in conflict resolution. It is only a third party that can take initiatives to determine parties and issues in relation to possible future conditions of conflict. Governments do not look many years ahead, and they are not likely to take initiatives in researching into or in solving future problems. This is the role of those studying problems of conflict, aware of theorising in this area, examining profiles of states that have and have not been engaged in conflicts, familiar with longer-term trends in world society, and prepared to predict continuation of some of these, and who can with some degree of credibility point to possible future sources of conflict and argue which policies should be avoided or should be encouraged if a condition of peaceful relations is to be maintained. This is a role traditionally filled by academics; it is one that could now be filled by recruited members of foreign offices and international institutions, thus including a 'third party' within decision making at national and international levels.

(i) FORECASTING

Conflict avoidance finally rests upon accurate forecasting, and forecasting is as yet an underdeveloped area of study. It will remain inadequate for practical purposes until more is known about the nature and processes of world society, and until increased data are available with which to measure trends.

Forecasting is not significant in government decision-making, particularly in party systems of government, outside the requirements of political objectives. There are both technical and political reasons for this. First, administrators advising governments are equipped to deal with aspects of future technical planning, for example, in relation to schools and hospitals, defence systems and roads. Forecasting outside such specific areas is not as yet within the competence of advisers: the independence demands of Asia and Africa were not anticipated after the Second World War, and participation demands within states still come as a surprise when they occur. What forecasting there is about future world conditions and responses of peoples and states merely reflects cultural and ideological attitudes, and historically derived expectations. Second, government decision-making is crisis decision-making: it is when decisions must be taken in respect of a particular matter that it comes to the attention of governments. Formal decision-makers are not accustomed to looking ahead, and to adjusting their day-to-day decision-making to future expectations. The problems Britain faces today in many parts of the world are a direct consequence of decisions taken many years ago, and many of these were taken at administrative levels. For administrative and procedural reasons, including overloading of decision-making, decisions at formal governmental level tend to deal with the problem at hand, with little opportunity to consider conditions likely to be created in the future by the decisions taken in respect of it. Third, this tendency is reinforced by political pressures. Immediate political needs are more important to politicians than the longer term consequences of their actions: governments look ahead to the next election more than to the ultimate consequences of their policies.

Scholars who have indulged in political forecasting have been little more successful than practitioners, and have been no less culturally and ideologically bound. Even estimates of population growth have been seriously in error. Changing values and expectations, and the self-fulfilling nature of some expectations are not readily assessed from any one culture. The subjective nature of forecasting was frankly confessed by Kahn and Wiener when they made their estimates of world conditions in the year 2,000.[1] Their tables of trends omitted some variables others would judge to be influential, if not decisive. However, confessing to sources of error does not remove them. The 'new techniques of the think tanks' are inadequate because they fail to overcome the limitations imposed on the thinkers by their own environments and experiences. Data collectors and manipulators arrive at misleading hypotheses when they fail to allow for the fact that relationships are perceived phenomena, and that perceived relationships have a self-creating tendency.

The theorising that has taken place about world society, for example, theorising about the role of the individual, the nature of social change and the consequences of communications, provides some of the basic hypotheses on which predictions might be made. But even the wholly coordinated scholarly knowledge available at any one time could provide no more than a starting point. The future is at least in part a consequence of expectations, and future relationships between peoples and states are at least in part the consequence of current perceptions of each other now, and of current perceptions of each other in the future. It is the projections of parties in any relationship that must be the guide to prediction. This subjective projection needs to be adjusted in the light of persistent trends and knowledge of environmental conditions. Consequently, the projection of relationships by parties concerned within a controlled academic framework that can supply available knowledge, offers a more reliable means of prediction than those that have until now been employed either by governments unilaterally, or by academics speculating from within one culture.

An example will help to make the point. Governments have called upon scholars to help them predict future world political conditions so that defence planning – which for technical reasons must be some ten years in advance of employment of defence systems – can be more relevant when put into use, and less costly as a result of obsolescence brought about by political changes. However, scholars cannot be useful except in predicting measurable phenomena and making studied judgements of trends. On the other hand, in the light of what knowledge they do have about world society, as for example about participation demands, technological developments and their consequences and altering values, they can help representatives of governments to focus on features in a particular region that might otherwise be overlooked, and draw out knowledge and insights possessed by governments the relevance of which to future conflicts are likely to be missed by them. The complicated ethnic relationships existing in the region that includes Malaysia, Indonesia and Singapore, which each of these governments tends to regard as being relevant only to domestic politics, cannot be regarded as irrelevant to their relationships in the seventies. A third party can pose questions, but the governments involved must give the answers. Similarly, ethnic, social and political elements in the Persian Gulf area need to be brought to the surface before prediction can be reliable; but it is only the parties that can do this with accuracy because the future includes perceived aspects. One of the great errors in decision-making in the contemporary world is due to greater powers making their estimates of future responses of other states on the basis of their own subjective assessment of the expectations of the peoples concerned. The United States acts in South East Asia on the 'domino' theory; but it has arrived at this theory with very little knowledge about the attitudes, fears, expectations and hopes of the peoples concerned, with very little apparent awareness of the nature of nationalism, and in its own perspective of a world threatened by Communism. A different defence strategy, and indeed a different attitude to governments in the area that are being accorded support, would probably emerge, if their future expectations of the more persistent movements and trends within the world political system were examined.

(ii) RACE CONFLICT

One of the major sources of future international conflict is current racial prejudice. At present this is thought to be primarily a matter of domestic politics; but it also operates internationally, and correlates in its incidence with the existence of problems of development. Just as there has been in the past a spill-over effect whenever forces opposing feudal governments have sought foreign assistance from others, so racial groups within states that experience discrimination will seek the support of other such groups, and of states with a sympathy for or interest in their cause. There will be reaction by groups and states that wish to preserve their positions. Already there is evidence of this spill-over from racial tension in the United States of America, the United Kingdom, Rhodesia, South Africa and the remaining colonial regions of Africa. It is taking place in a global background of increasing inequalities between states that have predominantly black and predominantly white populations.

Attention has already been drawn to the similarities between racial and class conflict. Indeed, communal racial conditions are characterised by occupational differences between races, and the attitudes and prejudices about morals, cleanliness and behaviour generally which are associated with class relations. Greek–Turkish, Malayan–Chinese, Fijian–Indian, Israeli–Arab economic and social relations are not unlike the class relations of Britain.

Where income and social status are high, race relationships provide no difficulties. Diplomats from all states meet on equal terms, as do scholars, entertainment stars, royalty and sportsmen, and professional workers usually have an equal status. Negroes in the United States who are successful professionally or academically frequently find themselves alienated from their ethnic 'class', so much so that some colleges have found difficulty in persuading Negroes to apply for admission to post-graduate classes.

However, whereas a black or white person can come from one social class, alter accent, dress and behaviour and be accepted in another, colour remains a permanent feature restricting social mobility. If all white persons from working class homes in Britain were branded on the face, social mobility would be reduced. It is probable that pigmentation alone creates the difference between racial tensions and communal conflict due to class and ideology. It is also probable that pigmentation is a less divisive factor than class or creed: it may be easier to achieve assimilation of different races of the one social group than different classes of the one ethnic group. If this were so then the policy objective would be to ensure that class and creed conflicts did not get confused with race conflicts in the minds of people, and in housing and other practices. For many reasons there is invariably a high correlation between black minorities and low social status in white communities, which tends to associate the two in the minds of observers. Equal educational, housing and other opportunities for social advancement are the appropriate means. However, communication between the groups to expose the nature of the problem as one of income and opportunity rather than one of race, and thus to offset prejudice, is necessary in order to provide the political background in which these policies can be advanced.

The more difficult problem to resolve is racial conflict within the one multi-racial income group: race prejudice is at its highest among unskilled workers. One reason is that the black immigrant worker is frequently more educated and cultured than the white worker in the same income group just because of discrimination which forces black workers to accept employment opportunities below their skills and abilities. A resentment is created which is the opposite from the general communal one where black citizens are held to be inferior, and is all the more bitter among those whites affected. Another reason is, of course, competition for scarce unskilled jobs.

These observations on domestic conflict are stimulated by observations made of international conflicts: some feed-back from micro-international studies to national social studies is to be expected. Perhaps some feed-back in means of handling conflict may also occur.

(iii) ADAPTED TECHNIQUES

The needs of research are understood or at least accepted by most governments, and a research framework is still the appropriate one for prediction. Government research or government sponsored research units are a possibility at the national level, especially if it can be shown that sub-stantial savings might result in defence planning and in avoidance of conflict situations that disrupt aviation and commerce. At the international level a research institution that can bring parties together who might in the future be in conflict, or are in a region of discontinuous change the consequences of which cannot easily be determined, could assist in forecasting. The desirable procedure is for states to meet at six-monthly intervals within a controlled communication framework, projecting three to four years ahead. Experience gained by governments and by scholars in one set of discussions would increase the probability of accurate forecasting in others, and would probably increase the efficiency of day-to-day decision-making generally.

In this current research project steps have been taken to examine the possibilities of prediction of relationships. (Some of the difficulties that have been encountered in achieving the cooperation of governments are referred to in the next chapter.) It has been found necessary in some cases to undertake discussions with only one state at a time, and this raises the difficulties experienced by a mediator who deals with only one party. Questions about relationships with other states and about relevant domestic political and social matters are quickly interpreted as revealing prejudice on the part of the academics present. One device attempted has been to agree in advance that questions likely to be regarded as hostile are put by one or two panel members, leaving the others free to act as a third party with a supportive role.

NOTE TO CHAPTER SEVEN

(1) Kahn and Wiener, *The Year 2000*.

8 Political Willingness to Resolve Conflict

However desirable it might seem that conflict should be settled, resolved or avoided, and however carefully devised might be the means available, the factor of political willingness to end and avoid conflict is a decisive one. There are three approaches to this problem of political willingness. There is, first, the normative view that parties to disputes should submit to means of peaceful settlement in accordance with the United Nations Charter and with general principles of law; second, the notion that conflict has a functional value in the maintenance of social unity and political development, and that parties cannot, therefore, be expected to try to terminate conflict while a functional value exists; and third, the hypothesis that political willingness to end and avoid conflict relates to the relevance of the procedures for peaceful settlement that are available in relation to the particular nature and stage of the dispute.

(i) THE NORMATIVE VIEW

The normative view implies a legal or moral obligation on the part of the states or parties involved to submit to third party interventions and decisions. There is in addition an implied obligation to make judicial and related processes work, in the general interests of world society. Those who hold this view are inclined to argue that the traditional processes of peaceful settlement of disputes, which are based upon tested municipal practices, are satisfactory provided that there is the political willingness to employ them. (It is this view which was advanced in the literature to be referred to in Chapter Ten.)

This is not unlike the view that peace would be assured if only states would disarm and agree to create an international organisation that had its own forces by which to implement its decisions. It is a view that dodges the main issues: it could be that the reason why universal collective security has not developed beyond legal theory, despite major attempts after two world wars, is that it is misconceived, and is not a proposal relevant to the needs and values of world society in which states are the main actors. A solution to any problem, be it mechanical, medical or organisational, must be relevant to the problem in all its aspects. When shoulds and oughts enter into argument it can be taken for granted that the remedies being offered do not stand on their own merits.

The justification for this normative attitude towards political willingness to accept third party decisions is an idealistic one. Parties enter into relationships, sometimes formalised by agreements, and are expected to act in accordance with their provisions. There are traditional, moral and normative reasons for this expectation. In municipal law penalties are imposed by third parties when agreements are broken, and the same conditions should apply, it is thought, in relations between international actors. The analogy of municipal law is, however, not a good one. Decision-makers of states enter into tacit or formal agreements, and their personal and ideological intentions are usually to carry them out. However, decision-makers are not individuals acting as persons and responsible only to themselves. They cannot be aware always of systemic and future needs, of the consequences of their policies, and of the various pressures that will be at play. A government might accept an agreement restricting the spread of nuclear weapons, and its members might like to see it work; but events could easily force it to break the agreement. Needs felt by leaders, idealistic hopes, intellectually satisfying programmes and well drafted agreements are not necessarily those required by systemic circumstances. Moral and normative influences cannot offset or condition systemic ones, and it is misleading to suggest that they could or should. A state that has agreed to a collective security system cannot accept the coercion of that system when applied to its own behaviour at some future date when its behaviour is designed in its view to protect some fundamental value. So it is with peaceful settlement of disputes; undertakings to make use of means provided, like undertakings never to resort to force, can be treated as binding only in so far as they appear relevant to the needs of the state concerned in the circumstances in which the state is reacting. Decisions by third parties, no matter how derived, cannot be accepted when they run counter to political and system needs.

The need for relevance in the forms of institutions has been underlined by theories of 'functionalism'. Functional institutions persist where there is a perceived interest in cooperation with them. There cannot be any coercive or punitive powers other than those which are inherent within membership and conditions of membership. There is, therefore, a clear distinction between legal and functional approaches. The former are based upon the belief that the provision of sensibly created institutions itself tends to induce behaviour that conforms with them: the League and the United Nations once created were intended to attract support and induce the behaviour set down in the agreed articles. The latter are based upon the belief that relevant institutions emerge out of behaviour: telecommunications arrangements, health agreements and the rules of navigation formalise patterns of behaviour either tacitly agreed previously, or from which all concerned gain on a reciprocal or convenience basis. Empirically the evidence is not in favour of the legal approach: the federal structures imposed on African states by foreign rulers have tended to disintegrate despite attempts by successor governments to maintain them, whereas federations, such as the Australian one, which were constitutional acceptances of transactions and relationships already evolving, and for which there was a political or felt need, have a high degree of stability. So, too, with procedures for the settlement of disputes: there is a political willingness to use them only to the extent that they appear to be relevant to the circumstances and the requirements of the parties.

Unwillingness to use certain procedures cannot be assumed to be an unwillingness to use any means, or a desire not to deal with the conflict in some constructive way. Nor can it be assumed that a rejection of the legal or normative approach is 'immoral', 'uncivilised' or 'anarchical' as is often implied, due probably to the fact that it is non-European states that have appeared least enthusiastic about the compulsory jurisdiction of the International Court – not even paying the lip service of Western states.[1] The procedures themselves are irrelevant to the needs they are designed to satisfy.

(ii) THE FUNCTIONAL VIEW

The belief that parties engage in conflict because they have some basic urge towards violence, because they see some political value in conflict, because of the nature of men and states, or for other natural and functional reasons, has always been widely reflected in political writings. (Functionalism of the Mitrany institutional type should not be confused with functional explanations of conflict as put forward by some sociologists.) This is not the occasion on which to review the biological and anthropological literature on the nature and origins of conflict, and the natural history of aggression. Sufficient has been said in this and in the companion study to suggest that, even though men and states were aggressive, even though states did perceive some value in conflict as a means of diverting attention away from awkward political problems, the resolution of conflict is still possible once alternative goals and means, and costs of conflict relative to these interests, have been considered and assessed.

Worthy of more serious consideration are the views of those scholars who suggest that conflict has a functional value to social systems implying that whatever might be the desires and ideologies of decision-makers, however well intentioned they might be in creating a League or a United Nations, conflict is likely to persist for systemic reasons, and that circumstances will therefore prevent the emergence of a political willingness to terminate conflict. It could reasonably be deduced from some of the propositions of Coser (formulated within a social and not an international context) that parties cannot be expected to settle conflicts by peaceful means where conflict has some integrative function, regardless of moral sanctions and the variety of means available.[2] More recently there have been some dramatic revelations from the 'Iron Mountain' which may or may not be taken seriously, but which even as parody reflect widespread attitudes for which there is support in the serious literature of sociology.[3]

The extrapolation from social behaviour to the behaviour of states in world society is attractive if only because it has for so long been general experience that states seem not to be interested in existing means of peaceful settlement of disputes, and because there appear to be no explanations of conflict other than the simply understood ones of natural causation. What biologists and sociologists have been doing, and what political commentators do, is to explain past behavioural patterns as though these patterns were fixed. There is an evolutionary or learning factor of which they are aware; but apart from this there is a factor which is inherent in systems behaviour to which less attention has been paid. Systems respond to an environment, and, moreover, in ways that seem appropriate at the time and in the light of information available. Environment and information alter. The patterns that have been assumed to be constant, and which have been explained in terms of instincts and functional necessity, are subject to change in the short term. If it is found that in some circumstances behaviour does not exhibit features that have been thought to be constant and inherent in social structures and processes, then this empirical evidence is sufficient to destroy the theory. It requires only one case of conflict resolution by learning processes to challenge the function theory of conflict. There is a tendency not to integrate empirical evidence in thought, and especially when it seems to be cutting the ground from under theories that are closely related to ideologies, such as an ideology that attributes social progress to the outcome of conflict.

There are, however, particular cases in which a functional value of conflict could reasonably be postulated, at least in the short term, even though it were agreed that conflict is subjective and not a systemic need, and can be avoided by reassessments of values and costs. These cases are those in which change demanded requires the total loss of positions of one party, as when social and political demands are made upon a colonial or feudal system. It is in these circumstances that violence is probably inevitable, and cannot be held to be dysfunctional, non-legitimised or in any sense immoral, and it is these circumstances that make important the distinctions made elsewhere between different types of conflict. Even cases such as these, however, are not different in kind from ones in which changed values lead to agreement. The difference lies only in levels of knowledge. The position of one feudal lord who is in complete control and will not brook social or political change and who can count upon foreign support, is different only in degree from the position of another who has assessed the forces of change and his inability to resist, and is prepared to adjust to them. There are differences of interest at any one time between groups that are interacting; but it cannot be deduced that conflict has a fundamental value, unless conflict is so broadly defined as to include any relationships in which subjective assessments of interest and values are undergoing change in response to changing environmental circumstances.[4]

(iii) WILLINGNESS AND PROCEDURES

It could be that the reason why some conflicts persist, and a reason why advantage is not taken of traditional means of peaceful settlement of disputes, is that these means are not appropriate or relevant to international society or the particular disputes. It could be that there is a direct connection between political willingness to settle, resolve or avoid disputes, and methods and opportunities by which this might be done.

Governments have shown themselves to be unwilling to submit political disputes to an international court. They are not prepared to run the risks of adverse judgements, or to be obligated to act in accordance with a verdict. They are more willing to submit to the processes of mediation. In cases in which they are not, the question has to be asked, why? There have been cases in which parties have been unwilling to cooperate with a United Nations mediator. Why? The problem may be to find the methods, techniques or structures in which parties are prepared to cooperate. Political willingness to avoid a conflict that is more costly than gains, to resolve and not just settle a conflict, is usually present: at least political leaders say it is present. If two parties are not prepared to meet face to face or take advantage of mediation, there is, then, some reason that appears to them to be sound: past experience of negotiation, fear of domestic repercussions, or others. There are very many known reasons why governments are reluctant to accept traditional third party interventions. These have been dealt with at length by Lall in his examination of the history of negotiation.[5] But evidence of and reasons for inflexibility of states that are involved in conflict are of limited analytical interest: they are part of the data which have to be taken into account. The inflexibility cannot be changed by exhortation, by appeal to moral responsibilities and by advocacy of 'civilised' methods of resolving conflict. Means have to be found that reduce inflexibility by being relevant to the conditions in which states operate. It is no defence of traditional method or of failure of mediation, merely to argue that there was an absence of political willingness on the part of governments to employ these methods.

This project has suggested the hypothesis that willingness and method are related. At least in some cases where traditional methods were not acceptable it was found that parties to disputes do wish to resolve them, and were prepared to enter into discussions that enabled them to explore the possibilities of resolution without risking having solutions imposed upon them. This academic framework, contrived for research reasons, seems to have been perceived by the conflicting parties involved as fashioning a new tool for use by parties seeking a resolution of conflict. Judicial processes are not believed to be relevant to political disputes that touch upon important interests and values. The less mandatory techniques of mediation and conciliation have most often failed to produce positive results, and have frequently seemed to lead to increased tensions. Diplomatic processes are those by which conflict has escalated, and may not always be available in its resolution or be considered useful. This academic framework, designed for research purposes, may have been perceived as a more acceptable technique that could be applied to the resolution of conflict. If this is so, it suggests that there may be circumstances in which states are eager to seek a resolution of conflicts in which they are involved, despite contrary theories of the functional nature of conflict, provided appropriate means can be devised.

It could be that cooperation in an academic project is a harmless act, and that there may be reasons of political expediency in seeming to want resolution of conflict, while making sure it is not resolved, in much the same way as great powers find it expedient to engage in disarmament discussions having made sure that their proposals are unacceptable to the other side. The evidence is against such a conclusion. First, the parties found value in discussions and sought their continuation after they were of decreased academic interest. In one case, in which it was generally believed that the conflict had a political value, discussions continued, usually at the request of the party alleged to have an interest in continuing the conflict, during a period of six months after the initial five days of discussion.

There have been found cases in which states were not prepared to cooperate in any traditional means of mediation, or in controlled communication. These are of particular interest because it is these, rather than cases in which controlled communication was possible even though other techniques had not proved possible, that throw light upon the problem of willingness.

(iv) REASONS FOR REJECTION OF CONTROLLED COMMUNICATION

For obvious reasons, it is not possible to name parties that were unwilling to cooperate in this project, but sufficient can be said to indicate patterns of response that emerged.

There were some cases where lack of cooperation was not wholly a matter of political willingness, and related more to fluidity in domestic politics, changes in government and anticipated changes. It takes time to communicate with each party, to follow up communications and obtain decisions, and then actually to arrange meetings. During this time there are internal and external political developments taking place, and the course of conflict is always changing. There was, in some instances, a change of government, or an election about to take place, just when all arrangements had been agreed for discussions. This was an academic project and communication facilities and local agents were not available to make the necessary approaches. Perhaps this is an aspect that could be overcome; but it would be misleading to treat every failure to come to the point of discussions as reflecting unwillingness on the part of the parties concerned. This probably applies to all means of peaceful settlement.

In addition to administrative problems there were expressed resistances that have very little to do with the problem of political willingness, and in particular the resistance of professionals and traditionalists who take the view that matters of international politics are of no concern to anyone except the states involved. Traditional attitudes act as a resistance to cooperation with the United Nations, and they provide an even greater resistance to interventions by unofficial third parties. In one case a refusal was found to be due to resistance from a foreign office that was affronted that there could be successful academic initiatives in a situation in which it had failed. In another case one party had already indicated its willingness to enter into controlled discussions, and the other party refused on grounds of protocol – the ordinary diplomatic channels were adequate, even though communication had to be through a protecting power, and the other party should make its own approach through ordinary channels. In such cases officials are reacting against an implication that the existence of the situation to be discussed might reflect upon their training, insights, and general efficiency, especially at a time like the present when advances in social sciences are in any event challenging them. Furthermore, practitioners in powerful states have difficulty in believing that their knowledge and perceptions might be faulty, or that their conflicts are not wholly due to the behaviour of the less responsible smaller powers. In practice, analysis of conflicts arising between smaller states involves larger ones, and there is less reluctance on the part of powerful states to participate as an interested party in an on-going discussion. In one case larger states demanded the right to participate. Thus, if smaller states submit a conflict to analysis, the larger powers with an interest in the conflict are induced to do the same.

In two other cases where there was greater power intervention in a local situation, there was an additional though not stated reason for not participating. Controlled communication provides for a searching analysis of motivations and interests, and the intervention of foreign states in a local conflict cannot readily be justified in terms usually employed in official public statements. The protection of the interests of one of the parties to the local dispute, a moral duty to prevent aggression anywhere in the world, and support for the principles of the United Nations, are acceptable as political rationalisations, but not in a situation in which the consequences of actions are being analysed by academics and by parties involved. Reluctance to enter into controlled discussions was symptomatic of policies that could not readily be justified except by reference to practices and values for the support of which there does not appear to be any clear world consensus.

Rejection was experienced wherever states were approached at a systems level higher than the local and original level of the conflict. Willingness is greatest at the lower systems levels, and least at higher levels where governments have some difficulty in claiming a direct interest, or do not wish to expose their motives. It could be argued that this is to be expected: greater powers would not submit their policies to analytical examinations when they were in a position to determine the outcome of the conflict. But this is an inadequate explanation. In the cases referred to, the greater powers were not in practice able to determine the outcome of the conflict: finally the initiative remained with the local parties. This situation is generally familiar. India and Pakistan could not be coerced into an agreement, and Greece and Turkey could not determine a solution to the Cypriot problem. The reasons why relatively greater powers are not willing to submit to controlled communication have to be sought in their own perception of the legitimisation of their behaviour.

This does not necessarily weaken the usefulness of controlled communication. On the contrary, it focuses attention on the need to approach a problem within a systems framework, and to commence at the local level. Perhaps some of the failure of traditional means has been due, not so much to the techniques, but to the tendency to give too much attention to the views of states that have no direct interest in the conflict at the local level. Once there is agreement at the local level, it is more difficult for other parties to exercise influence.

In practice, it is not always possible to arrange discussions at the local level, especially on matters of wider interest, for fear of reprisals or foreign intervention in some form designed to prevent agreement. In due course, however, when it has become clear that the foreign power is pursuing its own interests and not those of the party it purports to support, and that there can be no end to violence until there is local agreement, first the local parties are more defiant, and finally the foreign power welcomes a means of breaking off the struggle.

In many cases of conflict there is a constitutional problem which prevents mediation or conciliation. Currently West Germany does not admit the sovereign existence of East Germany, Arab States do not acknowledge the government of Israel, and the United States and South Vietnam governments do not regard the National Liberation

Front as a party principal in the conflict. No attempts to mediate between governments can succeed in such cases. In these cases the parties to disputes are not the *de facto* or *de jure* governments: they are communities. The problem is, basically, not constitutional – constitutional disputes are merely a symptom or a form conflict takes. The basic problem is in the relations between communities. Leaders of communities are usually prepared to communicate: there is a recognition of the physical existence of communities even though there is no recognition of the constitutional authorities. Face-to-face techniques are concerned with discussion of attitudes and perceptions, and the constitutional status of parties, whether they are recognised or not, is irrelevant because it is superficial. Insistence upon legally legitimised status, and refusal to recognise sociologically legitimised status, prevents communication. It usually reflects a sense of political weakness on the part of the legally legitimised authority. The parties to communication must be those who are in fact in conflict, and it is not always or even mostly that these are governments.

There is one aspect of political willingness that is far from clear. It does seem that some degree of escalation of conflict must occur once violence has taken place. One is tempted to refer to the phenomenon of blood-letting before festive celebrations with which anthropologists are familiar. The reason seems to be that misperceptions, and false calculations of costs in relation to values occur, and this having happened, political rationalisation must take place to justify the result. Additional values are added to justify the rising costs: the United States discovered that it was saving freedom everywhere by fighting in Vietnam. It is only when escalation has occurred to an extent that makes obvious the disparity between costs and values at stake that there is political pressure for ending the conflict. There appear to be stages in conflicts at which discussion between the parties seems to be irrelevant to them. For this reason conflict avoidance is all the more important: a threshold is crossed once violence occurs.

This limited evidence would seem to suggest that the legal and functional approaches should be modified at least to take into account the possible relevance of other procedures. The legal approach reflects unstated notions about world society and conflict, and the functional approach is essentially an attempt to explain the reasons why conflict has been a persistent feature of societies, and reflects the same naturalist thinking of the historians, philosophers and lawyers of the past. This approach, which suggests that procedures might be relevant, no less reflects a body of theory and assumptions. The interaction between experience in the resolution of conflict, on the one hand, and theories concerning world society and conflict on the other, is only now commencing. It is beginning to offer areas of enquiry more interesting academically and politically than do either normative or functional approaches to conflict. Its extension into forecasting will add to knowledge both of procedures and of the operations of world society. Among the many and varied topics that appear to be relevant and to invite research are the consequences of foreign support to parties in disputes, questions of legitimacy and consensus, the connections between domestic and international conflict, the influence of racial and class prejudice, the functional value of conflict and legitimacy of conflict in conditions in which power is employed as a substitute for adjustment to demands for change, the importance of proficiency in decision-making, and the limited role of coercive international institutions. These and many other similar areas of enquiry which emerge out of a behavioural approach to world society suggest at least the possibility that we need not be content merely with the enforced settlements of disputes in a world system organised by relative power relations.

(v) POLITICAL WILLINGNESS AND CONFLICT AVOIDANCE

Some special problems arise when the problem is conflict avoidance, and not conflict resolution. In particular there is a first reaction that even to discuss conflict avoidance is prejudicial to relationships because of the implied expectation of conflict. Even states that are engaged in a local arms race are inclined to deny the existence of any conflict problem. Indeed, states that are in practice in an escalating conflict relationship are understandably less inclined to bring their fears to the surface in the presence of each other than are others that enjoy harmonious relationships. Yet it is they that can gain most by endeavouring to avoid conflict by means other than an (escalating) arms parity.

In some circumstances there are *a priori* reasons for anticipating conflict situations, as when it is known that sudden change will take place in a particular region. When the United Kingdom government announced in 1968 its policy decision to withdraw from the Far East and the Persian Gulf in the early seventies, anxieties and fears, concern about 'power vacuums', the possible interventions of other powers, and the dangers of racial or ideological conflicts, could be anticipated. A reasonable assumption would be that sudden change of this character could promote situations of tension. An initiative to arrange for an analysis of projected relationships could not be regarded as creating conflict by anticipating it. Nevertheless, even in circumstances such as these states are reluctant to discuss their hopes and aims openly, at least until they have assessed possibilities and have established their claims in the new circumstances. By this time a conflict situation is likely to have been created.

In the context of conflict avoidance the professional jealousies already noted are even more pronounced. Officials and governments that have been through various forms of mediation and are still involved in dysfunctional conflict can be persuaded to try different approaches, and to accept that some problems require assistance from many different agencies. Conflict avoidance, however, is closely related to day-to-day decision-making. The practitioners are the 'experts', and in their view others are not in a position to point to significant features that have not already been taken into account. It is for these reasons that the device, already referred to, of meeting with the representatives of one state separately, has been found to be necessary: the 'expert' does not object to being a source of information.

NOTES TO CHAPTER EIGHT

(1) See Higgins, *Conflict of Interests*, p. 90 ff.
(2) Coser, *The Functions of Social Conflict.*
(3) Lewin (ed.) *Report from Iron Mountain on the Possibility and Desirability of Peace.*
(4) See on this topic Coser, *Continuities in the Study of Social Conflict.*
(5) Lall, *Modern International Negotiation.*

PART TWO

ASSESSMENT

9 Trends in the Analysis of World Society

It was stated in the Introduction that while conflict resolution by controlled communication might be of greater interest, the original purpose of the technique was to throw light upon the nature of relations between parties in conflict, and by this means, on to the nature of world society. In this and the subsequent chapter separate reviews are made, first of approaches to the study of international politics, and second to the handling of conflicts. It will be seen that controlled communication is the logical extension of trends in both fields, thus providing a meeting point of analysis of world society and the study of conflict resolution.

Political scientists have recently been looking back on the development of international studies, trying to absorb the great flow of ideas of the last decade or so by classifying them, and trying to detect common directions and trends of thought throughout the whole history of thought in this area. For example, Harrison has pointed to four stages of growth: the period before the First World War when diplomatic history was the main content of studies; the post-war period in which there was great interest in law and in international institutions as a problem solver; the period of the depression and after when current events and the immediate present held the attention of political observers; and the period since the Second World War in which scholars have concentrated their attention upon the underlying forces in international politics.[1] Thompson has observed another growth pattern: he described the successive stages as the legal approach, the political approach, the institutional approach, and the later concentration upon multilateral diplomacy in all its aspects.[2] Quincy Wright has perceived a shift in thinking since the Middle Ages from the politics, institutions and practices of imperialism when the world was perceived as a plan, to the period of nationalism when equilibrium was of interest, to internationalism when organisation was the object of attention, and to the more neutral study of the world as a 'field' in which the behaviour of government, states, nations and people is analysed.[3]

The main trend that these and other writers discern seems to be from the study of the general towards the study of the particular. Accompanying this is a trend from description towards analysis. In the last few years the same trends have led to increased attention being given to micro-analysis, detailed studies of decision-making, systems analysis and the use of controlled or laboratory situations that enable testing of hypotheses and quantitative approaches. Generally speaking, the scholarly struggle to be more precise has been a struggle to overcome the difficulties inherent in the subject matter. First the data of a situation or event that is being analysed must approximate reality; but recorded observations are many steps removed from reality. Second, the data need to be complete; but recorded observations represent merely a selection. When the political scientist tries to overcome these problems by methods adopted by physical sciences, that is, by abstracting from reality, by placing some aspects of international politics in a laboratory situation, and by examining variables under controlled conditions, then the problem of relating the abstraction to reality has to be overcome. It is possible to isolate some physical and chemical interactions and to observe them, but it is usually misleading to isolate behavioural responses. Different approaches have been employed to overcome these difficulties. It is the historical succession of these approaches, the nature and completeness of evidence, and the methods by which data are generated, with which we are now concerned.

(i) THE HISTORICAL APPROACH

An event, which may be a period of world history or a particular regional happening, a crisis, or even a decision, has in the perspective of an observer an infinite number of features. No matter how short is the time involved, the potential data are infinite; a full and complete description of a day in one's life or of the interactions within a small group meeting for an hour is impossible because the details are infinite – for example, movements, facial expressions and thoughts. An event, therefore, cannot be described completely. The raw material of an historical event includes the physical evidences that remain, records of all kinds including contemporary official documents and unofficial accounts, art works, and any other contemporary records. What is thus recorded is a finite amount; it is possible theoretically (and more and more in practice with the aid of electronic devices) to take into account every detail contained in these records. The gap between the infinite details of the original event and the finite records represents that great proportion of the total event that contemporary spokesmen and observers did not believe to be sufficiently significant or relevant to record, or was not perceived at all by them.

In practice, many details are eliminated deliberately from the original records, and many others sub-consciously, even though they may have been known to be important; official explanations of events and policies do not always reflect the real ones. Press correspondents and contemporary observers select facts and report on the basis of their own preconceived notions, and the demands of their audiences. Thus, even the raw material of history is likely to be inadequate and misleading; the further one goes back into history, the fewer are the records, and the smaller is the finite selection of details.

However much smaller might be the content of records as compared with the event, it is still a large mass. The historian has the task of reducing this finite quantity of detail to readable proportions, and he must engage upon a selection process so as to include only what he thinks most relevant. He, like the observer of the event, selects according to his interests, assumptions and theories and these vary from age to age no less than from person to person in any one age.

The next stage in building a history is for the synoptic historian to take historical accounts of particular events and to select in such a way as to include some thousands of years of human activity into one or a few volumes. The basis of selection is cultivated judgement, a kind of trial and error or considered hunch, but not a training in social theories; for example, theories regarding the influence of a person on the role he enacts. The historian and the synoptic historian may manage to select so as to give a reliable impressionist picture of the past. It seems unlikely having in mind the process; but it could be if their theoretical insights were adequate. We do not know because there can be no testing short of prediction based upon theories derived from history, and self-fulfilling processes ensure that these can never be conclusive.

Having in mind the continuing selection process and the way in which details of behaviour and motivations tend to be lost in records, it is understandable that philosophers attempted to use their observations and reasoning to fill in some of the gaps in the historical account. Waltz has conveniently summarised some political philosophy in a way designed to make meaningful and useful the theories of the early political philosophers which 'are bewildering in their variety and contradictory qualities'.[4] He has made three broad divisions: first, those like St Augustine and Spinoza, who, as Morgenthau and Niebuhr later, found the causes of war in the nature and behaviour of Man: second, those like Plato, Kant and Bentham, who found the basic causes of conflict in the political structures, and the social and economic conditions of separate states; and third, those like Rousseau and James Mill, who found the major causes neither in men nor the state but in the international system based on states. Not unexpectedly the hypotheses of the political philosopher were not appreciably more precise than those of the historian; the difference was that the philosopher was deliberately searching for theories, and more consciously introspected regarding his own hypotheses. In the main these were normative theories, theories about how best to achieve certain goals, to obtain the good life, peace or freedom. They were, nevertheless, stimulating because they were exploratory and displayed great insight; all aspects of behaviour were within the realm of philosophy, and were conceptualised

as a whole, thus adding to the quantity of data taken into
account.

(iii) THE INSTITUTIONAL AND LEGAL APPROACH

World War I seemed to confirm the views of many
nineteenth-century thinkers who believed that international organisation was the only way of controlling state
behaviour, and that this needed to be of a type which
commanded means of centralised enforcement. Interest
was diverted from causes of war to means of suppressing
aggressive behaviour—this was the purpose of the League
Covenant. It was a period that provided an extensive
literature dwelling upon the nature of man, and the need
to introduce into world society the controls of municipal
society. Attention was focused upon some aspects of
world society, especially inter-state relations and the competitive power relations of states. Later thought was given
to functionalism as a form of noncoercive international
organisation. In the thirties Mitrany put forward a general
theory of functionalism which he subsequently developed,[5]
and which Claude[6] and Haas,[7] amongst others, have
employed. The emphasis was upon voluntary cooperation
in special activities which would promote improved
relationships in more sensitive areas. World War II and
the United Nations Charter gave added impetus to
institutionalists of both kinds – those interested in
coercive and those interested in cooperative forms.

(iv) SPECIALISATIONS

The war-promoted interest in institutions, and specialisation in science generally, to a large extent pushed aside political philosophy, speculative visions and ideal forms of

human life. Early in this century behavioural studies were formally structured as history, jurisprudence, political science, economics, psychology, anthropology, sociology and education – to name only some of the more important divisions: the total range of human activity was separated into defined behavioural patterns. Economic man had economic responses, and primitive society had its own special characteristics. Subjects were accorded boundaries within universities, and separate disciplines emerged.

The contribution to International Politics of these specialisations was, however, very little less speculative than the thinking of the philosophers; there could not be any testing of their theories in the international field. Moreover, even a hypothesis adequately tested on the individual or the small group could not be applied (except as analogy in order to explain a hypothesis) to the behaviour of states. Consequently, the major contribution that specialists in the social disciplines could make to International Relations was a methodological one, and in particular the results of their experience in adapting natural-science techniques to the requirements of the social sciences. A literature developed around the subject of method, and emphasis was placed on the need to test hypotheses.[8]

(v) FUNCTIONAL SPECIALISATIONS

As each social science advanced in its own special area of studies and as sociology developed as a separate discipline, the need was felt for interdisciplinary approaches to social phenomena. It was the common experience of scholars that one aspect of behaviour could not be explained without reference to others. There was, in this sense, a return to the earlier philosophic approach, or at least to a recognition of the value of an approach unconfined by specialisation. A different structure of social studies emerged. New studies cut across the boundaries of the older disciplines, and provided new perspectives. Social studies became structured into separate studies each of which had a bearing upon all the older specialisations: information theory, cybernetics, linguistics, sign behaviour, game theory, decision-making theory, value inquiry, change theory, operational research and general systems theory. These new disciplines fed back into the older ones and altered them further; the demarcation lines of the older behavioural disciplines became even more blurred, and their methods altered to cope with the problems of increased variables.[9]

In this development the social studies were influenced by the same intellectual and environmental circumstances that altered in a similar way the physical and biological sciences. The development was associated with movements from description to analysis, from personal preference to cause and effect, from statics to dynamics, from postulating to testing, from art to science. Indeed, this new structuring blurred the formerly clear demarcation lines that separated the natural sciences from the behavioural sciences; these older and more precise sciences shared the same methodological problems of which behavioural scientists were so much aware. They were similarly searching for general theories, and they similarly were required to question and to modify established laws and previously ascertained data.

International relations has been in a special position. Traditionally it was not a behavioural study: the analogies used by its theoretical expositors were mechanical and physical ones, focusing attention upon power and power balances, and doing this most usually by reference to historical situations already recorded in these non-behavioural terms. It became a behavioural study thanks to the development of studies in other fields. Being the behavioural study relevant to all behavioural relations between states, it necessarily borrowed terminology and methodology from all the structured social disciplines: the economic, psychological, historical and legal aspects of international relations were separate aspects of the whole. Now international relations is undergoing the same transition as are other social sciences; along with them it is breaking down boundaries that made it a field of study separate from other social sciences, and separate from physical sciences. Indeed, it has gained more than other studies for it has rid itself not only of the arbitrary structuring of social studies, but also of the additional arbitrary separation of international from other behaviour. The sociology of conflict is of increasing importance to international studies. Many of the methodological problems which international relations faced, by reason of being interdisciplinary and separate from the study of other aspects of social life, are now being avoided by greater reliance upon the newer studies that cut across the boundaries of the older disciplines. The dividing line between politics and international politics is difficult to determine.

One advantage of this newer structuring is that some hypotheses and special studies that could not be confined to any one discipline can now receive more adequate attention within a framework in which they have their special place. For example, the concept of power, one of the most discussed of all behavioural concepts, is now receiving renewed interest along with communications and other behavioural processes; in this new perspective it can be analysed as a means employed to achieve varieties of goals when communication and decision-making processes are inadequate or overloaded. Power theories, originally put forward in the context of traditional society, can now be restated in terms which might better explain contemporary conditions.

Thus we have two specialisation structures; the subject specialisations that evolved as more intensive studies were made of psychological, economic and other aspects of behaviour, and cutting across all these, functional specialisations that evolved as more interdisciplinary integration was seen to be necessary. Clearly no subject specialisation can provide a general theory of behaviour, but power, communications, cybernetics, functionalism, and other processes that cut across all, provide a valuable body of theory that serves as a basis for deductive reasoning.

(vi) GENERAL THEORISING

General theorising was promoted, first by the felt need to adopt interdisciplinary approaches, and second by the opportunities provided by the introduction of functional specialisations that cut across the social science disciplines. General theorising, the fourth stage in Harrison's sequence, relates more directly to the approach of political philosophy than to historical and institutional approaches. The historical and institutional studies seem, in retrospect, to have been an insertion into a flow of thinking, brought about by the temporary environmental conditions of two world wars. Their influence on contemporary thinking seems to be waning whereas the influence of earlier political thought remains significant. The political philosopher, the partial and the general theorist represent three historical stages in the evolution of political science, and international relations studies in particular. The contemporary general theorist is a political philosopher, but with the advantage of a background of the social sciences that provided partial theories, and of tested hypotheses concerning many aspects of social evolution and political behaviour.

(vii) GENERATION OF DATA

One reason why political scientists have confined themselves so much to general and historical studies and to theorising, is that international politics do not lend themselves to academic participation. The political scientist has had to be content with observing from afar; historical, philosophical and theoretical approaches have been convenient. On the other hand, the practitioner has not been interested in research; he has been too absorbed in day-to-day routines to think about how systems operate and why they fail. It has been easier and more expedient for him to use available power, even force, to control politics once there has been breakdown: the failure of his policy to achieve its goals by peaceful means has seemed to justify the use of power. From the practitioner's point of view the breakdown which required him to employ force was not of his own doing; it was the irrationality, or the aggressiveness, or in some other way the responsibility of other parties. No research, no questioning of traditional assumptions regarding international relations, has seemed necessary to him.

Recently, however, scholars have attempted to move nearer to the subject matter, despite the official monopoly over diplomacy. They have attempted to simulate situations – to enact different decision-making roles – and generally to get inside the shoes of the decision-makers. They have even played at games, like chess and poker, to obtain insights into bargaining, strategic and other decision-making processes. The scholarly tradition has been to rely upon documented evidence; but the modern historian has analysed in minute detail, and with mechanical and electronic aids, the contents of the documents of past periods, hoping by this means to find out more about the motives, responses and thought processes that lay behind the verbal behaviour of those who were making decisions. The new tools available for the processing of data have avoided some of the need to make personal selections of a few features that seemed relevant. In short, deprived of operational opportunities, scholars have, as a second best, tried to create situations for themselves and to use past situations better.

Simulation was described by one of its more imaginative promoters, Guetzkow, as 'an operating representation of central features of reality'.[10] It is the use of human subjects under quasi-laboratory conditions to create replicas of complex organisations, systems, and social processes; the use of human subjects in non-laboratory but contrived 'natural' settings for the above purposes, and use of machines experimentally to simulate mental and social processes as well as social systems.[11] Simulation is an old technique, used in ancient times by designers and model builders, in modern times as a teaching aid in legal studies, as a means of staff selection, and in many other ways. Its application and special development in the field of international studies is novel, and a direct result of the inaccessibility of the subject. Gaming, sometimes used synonymously,[12] is a particular form of simulation, the game being constructed to suit the special needs of some enquiry. In both cases the data are complete – a whole situation is being investigated; and in both cases the data are unreal, though with varying degrees of similarity with real conditions.

An approach that is more conventional, in that it takes the historical records as its source material, but radical in its techniques, is Content Analysis. This has been described by Osgood as an 'attempt to infer the characteristics and intentions of sources from inspection of the messages they produce'.[13] Content analysis is the usual method of historians, but as now developed it attempts to measure the intensity and frequency of responses in such detail as to justify the description 'behavioural'.[14] It, like the methods described above, attempts to add to the data usually available. In so far as it is dealing with real data on an increased scale, it is an advance on other methods.

These academic devices are not unlike those once used by the biologists, who, lacking research opportunities in faraway countries and in past situations of evolution, studied animal behaviour in zoos; and those used by social psychologists, who, lacking the resources necessary for large-scale investigation, made studies of small groups in gaols and other artificial situations. Some insights can be gained by these means; certainly data can be generated. But these controlled studies are misleading because the data generating process is only a second best. This is now clear in the case of animal behaviour; with resources available for field work, especially photographic equipment, discoveries have been made that challenge the conclusions arrived at by observation of behaviour in artificial conditions.

Face-to-face interaction within a controlled situation could be regarded as a form of simulation in that it generates its own data and involves 'the use of human subjects in non-laboratory but contrived "natural" settings'. It could also be regarded as an extension of content analysis in that in addition to generating its own data it requires the same detailed analysis of data generated.

However, it is one step nearer still to the subject matter.

(viii) FIELD WORK

Once there is a departure from historical and philosophical studies, once there is an interest in processes and the details of behaviour, field work suggests itself. Field work and controlled communication interact: work by one method suggests areas of enquiry by the other. Prior to an exercise in controlled communication it is necessary to be aware of the relevant geo-political influences and the general background of the dispute. During controlled communication attention is directed to social and political questions, the answers to which can be obtained only by field work. For example, in a communal conflict in which claims are made of communal incompatibility and counter-claims of possible community integration, an examination is required of incidents of violence in relation to different sizes of minorities involved.

Field work, empirical studies and the detailed descriptive studies to which they lead, are recent developments in the study of international relations—despite their widespread use in anthropology and sociology. There have been area studies, but most have been almost journalistic accounts of state policies and relationships. There have more recently been surveys of public attitudes.[15] There are still few cases of controlled observation such as that of Alger in relation to international institutions, and inter-actions within them.[16] Simulation, content analysis, controlled communication, and other devices that generate data and hypotheses are forcing scholars in this area of studies to rely less upon historical analysis, and more upon direct observation within a framework of pre-theorising, and upon the testing of propositions by these means.

(ix) PROCESSING OF DATA

Generation of data by these various techniques and by field work takes the study of world society little further than more traditional methods unless the data can be processed, and hypotheses examined by means which bring to attention the variables that are significant. Data generated or acquired have to be translated into a usable form,[17] data processing is a technique as important as the means by which the information was obtained,[18] and factor analysis and probability theory are among the essential tools of the political scientist.

Here we face some special problems. Simulation and content analysis make available a finite number of data, and processing is practicable. Once we move a step nearer to a real situation, as is the case with controlled communication, some additional problems are involved. The situation cannot be observed without changing it, and the opportunities of recording are limited. There is the possibility that controlled communication as a research technique has some of the weaknesses associated with observation of reality as conducted by historians and political philosophers: there are difficulties in arranging a sufficient degree of control to make possible accurate observation of variables.

In summary, the history of thought in international relations has been a history of struggle to maximise data – or to minimise selection – and to employ 'real' as distinct from 'simulated' sources of data. Controlled communication is a logical extension of this struggle.

Recent trends in general theorising, trends towards empirical work and more rigorous processing of data, do not represent a passing fashion, or merely an exercise in greater elegance of exposition, but an interdisciplinary reaction against specialisation, and a marrying of philosophy and science. On the evidence of other behavioural studies, the future in international relations will be characterised by improved theorising and more empirical work, with the emphasis on the testing of hypotheses. Simulation, content analysis, and controlled communication are not extraneous insertions into the flow of thought in this area of studies: they are integral parts of an historical trend from an art to an applied science.[19]

NOTES TO CHAPTER NINE

(1) Harrison (ed.), *The Role of Theory in International Relations.*
(2) See in Harrison, ibid.
(3) Ibid.
(4) Waltz, *Man, the State and War* and his chapter in Fox (ed.), *Theoretical Aspects of International Relations.*
(5) Mitrany, *A Working Peace System.*
(6) Claude, *Swords into Plowshares.*
(7) Haas, *Beyond the Nation-State.*
(8) See MacIver, *Social Causation;* Skinner, *Science and Human Behaviour;* Popper, *The Poverty of Historicism;* Kerlinger, *Foundations of Behavioral Research.*
(9) See for a general review of developments in the behavioural studies, Handy and Kurtz, *A Current Appraisal of the Behavioral Sciences.*
(10) Guetzkow (ed.), *Simulation in International Relations*, p. 25.
(11) Snyder, ibid, pp. 2–3.
(12) Ibid, p. 2.
(13) See Suci, Tannenbaum, *The Measurement of Meaning*, p. 275.
(14) See North, Holsti, Zaninovich, Zinnes, *Content Analysis.*
(15) See in Kelman, *International Behavior.*

(16) Alger, 'Interaction in a Committee of the United Nations General Assembly'.

(17) See Singer, 'Data-Making in International Relations'.

(18) See Janda, *Data Processing*.

(19) See Meehan, *The Theory and Method of Political Analysis* for an important contribution in this area.

10 Trends in the Control of Conflict

So far we have been concerned with trends in the study of world society in order to explain the use of the technique of face-to-face communication as an analytical device. Now we turn to examine some trends in the management of world society to explain the relevance of this technique in the avoidance and resolution of conflict.

The inadequacies of traditional means of peaceful settlement are widely acknowledged, and have been substantiated by a survey of past instances of adjudication, arbitration, mediation and conciliation in the peaceful settlement of international disputes.[1] Students with ideological attachments to international institutions, wedded to legal approaches as an ultimate solution, or driven by a faith that upholding an ideal will help to promote it, find evidence of success in the use of these processes, at least enough to defend them. Coldly appraised a degree of success sufficient to meet the needs of world order cannot be claimed. However, it is not instructive to argue over degrees of success generally or in relation to particular situations. What is required in addition to empirical studies of peaceful settlement of disputes is an examination of theoretical and practical possibilities, calling upon past experience, favourable or unfavourable, merely for purposes of illustration.

A study group was set up in 1963 by the David Davies Memorial Institute for International Studies to examine the peaceful settlement of international disputes. Its membership ensured a serious and thoughtful analysis, and the views expressed represented conventional wisdom and informed opinion on this subject.[2] The striking feature of the report is the way in which the group was pulled in two different directions. On the one hand confidence in judicial processes was affirmed and reaffirmed; on the other there was a realistic acknowledgement that they had failed.

> The members of the Group yield to no one in the importance which they attach to the judicial process as a means of peaceful settlement and also as a means of clarifying and developing international law. On the other hand, they recognise that the legal relations between states are more complex than those between individuals and that judicial settlement cannot be expected – at any rate in the near future – to play so large a role in the international community as in national systems.[3]

They sought a solution to their intellectual dilemma by suggesting greater employment of less formal procedures. 'In the past, they suspect, the best may have been the enemy of the good in the sense that, by placing so much emphasis on acceptance of compulsory jurisdiction, lawyers and statesmen may to some extent have overlooked the possibility of making more immediate progress through the lesser and more flexible procedures of inquiry, mediation and conciliation.'[4] They further supported their position by implying that there was nothing fundamentally inadequate in judicial procedures; the problem was a lack of willingness on the part of states to submit to voluntary or compulsory third party determinations: 'when the existing machinery and procedures are taken as a whole, there can be little doubt that they furnish any states willing to use them with effective means of peaceful settlement. The techniques of mediation, conciliation, arbitration and judicial settlement are highly developed, and their procedures stand comparison with those used in national systems'.[5] At the same time the group acknowledged the particular difficulties associated with traditional means of peaceful settlement, and the existence of the general problem of freedom of action that is likely to persist and which inhibits states from accepting not only judicial processes but even less formal ones. 'This freedom, if not lost, is hampered in ascending degree by good offices, inquiry, mediation and conciliation; and with arbitration, judicial settlement and conciliation of the binding type it is surrendered.'[6] The group did not deal with a reasonable hypothesis that the deficiencies in these means of settlement might never be overcome if the processes were not relevant to the nature of world society.

A short description of each of the traditional techniques of peaceful settlement of disputes will help to explain the relevance of controlled communication, and its similarities with and differences from more conventional processes. They are presented in descending order of third party coercion and intervention, and ascending order of participation by the parties involved in the dispute.

(i) JUDICIAL PROCESSES

Judicial processes are superficially quite different from the less formal procedures of negotiation, and for this reason invoke different responses from states. Once entered upon, judicial procedures remove the ultimate power of decision from states, and in respect of disputes involving political considerations this is usually unacceptable to states. Not only is the power of decision removed; it is transferred to an authority whose responses cannot reliably be forecast and whose guide-lines are far from clear, and when clear not always thought to be relevant. The views of the study group referred to above are an appeal rather than a description of reality.

> If these doubts are understandable and need to be alleviated by all possible means, they scarcely seem to justify a wholesale distrust of the judicial process, while their weight must tend to diminish with every year that passes. They do not appear to justify wholesale distrust of the judicial process because the fundamental principles and the general body of international laws have their roots in the essential nature of inter-state relations and the considerations which led to their formation have a value which is independent of the particular historical conditions in which they were created. Consequently, they have as much importance for new as for old states, and for the most part there has not been any disposition to question them.[7]

It may be that fundamental principles are not questioned only because they are not considered relevant, or because they are so vague in relation to a particular circumstance that they cannot be questioned.

Apart, however, from the much discussed problems of willingness and uncertainty of law, the judicial process suffers from some practical difficulties, some of which are real even though not essential to judicial processes. For example, disputes between communities within a state, be they ethnic or ideological, cannot easily be brought before an international court, yet there is evidence that international conflicts may have their origin in communal conflicts.[8] Conflict avoidance is probably a more important process than conflict settlement, and judicial processes can make little contribution to it. Furthermore, judicial settlements must be confined to some degree to legal questions if courts are not to be given wide discretionary powers that might further inhibit reference of disputes by states.

Furthermore, judicial processes are not usually successful in solving problems posed by change. On the contrary, they tend to consolidate existing values and institutions just because decisions are based upon past practices. Any attempt to widen the decision-making role of courts to take into account altered values makes a political legislature of courts, and no state would find this acceptable. The result is that the judicial process when applied to a political dispute is likely to leave at least one party dissatisfied, and could leave all parties with a grievance, thus continuing or creating a new conflict situation. In short, judicial processes are coercive at least in the sense that there are political and social sanctions even in the absence of enforcement procedures. They assume that disputes are over objective conflicts of interest in which the gain of one party is the loss of another, and they inhibit exploration of alternative solutions.

(ii) ARBITRATION

By arbitration is meant 'the settlement of a dispute by the award of a tribunal which gives effect to existing law and which binds the parties'.[9] Unlike judicial processes arbitration can more readily take into account non-legal argument. It can also take place in secret. It commits parties less, though custom is that its findings are as binding as those of judicial processes. Its procedures can be more flexible, even though attempts are made to follow the practices of law in the giving and sifting of evidence. The confidence of the parties in the decision-maker is established by the custom of selection of the arbitrator by the parties. It is one step away from judicial processes toward the other extreme of direct negotiation. As such it suffers from many of the drawbacks of judicial processes, and has few of the advantages of greater participation by the parties in the making of decisions.

It is not implied that judicial and quasi-judicial processes cannot be relevant and effective. It may be that the conventional view that issues of high political content are not referred to judicial settlement because of the uncertainties of the judicial process cannot be substantiated by empirical evidence. The Indian–Pakistani dispute over the Rann of Kutch seemed to be settled by arbitration in 1967. We do not know which types of disputes are likely to be settled by judicial process, or in what circumstances. Perhaps it is not the judicial nature of the procedures that has made states resistant. It could, for example, be the composition of the judiciary. Nor do we know how arbitration decisions are made, in particular why some non-legal considerations are taken into account and not others, and the reaction of states to this wider or more overt process of subjective judgement. These matters are the subject of a separate study being undertaken by this Centre; the potential of controlled communication cannot be assessed adequately without more knowledge of the potential of and resistance to other methods.

(iii) CONCILIATION

Conciliation is a term used to imply a closer relationship to the parties on the part of the third party than is implied by arbitration. While judicial procedures and arbitration are concerned with settlement of disputes and the allocation of values according to past practices, conciliation is concerned with activities that help to lead the parties to agreement. These activities could include endeavours to obtain and to clarify facts, and to check assertions. It is an active rather than interpretative role. The examination of the dispute could lead to recommendations, and even to formal findings which parties might be expected to accept. The success or failure of conciliation relates in some degree to the relations established between conciliator and the parties, which is not the case with judicial processes.

The inherent dangers of 'fact-finding' by a third party need to be noted. 'Facts' in any dispute are perceived differently by the parties, and activity by a third party is likely to destroy relationships between it and the conflicting parties. Experience is that states involved in disputes resist fact-finding activities by institutions and third parties. Any active role by the third party, be it ascertaining the 'facts', making suggestions, or in any way bringing pressure to bear, is likely to destroy the effectiveness of the conciliation it was designed to achieve just because the interests of one party are likely to be prejudiced. The role of the conciliator is no more than the term implies, the role of pacifying, or trying to ensure that parties do not react against each other, but take time to consider their response. It is a departure from legal processes: history, law, morality, expediency are all relevant as factors to be taken into account, but they are taken into account by the parties with no more than recommendation and suggestion by the conciliator.

(iv) MEDIATION

Mediation implies the participation of a third party in negotiations between the parties. It is different from judicial procedures in that it serves negotiation, and there is less activity or intervention by the third party than in conciliation. The role of the mediator is to present the case of the parties to each other. In practice, mediation is usually applied in circumstances in which the parties are not willing to meet to negotiate, or to meet with a conciliator. Thus mediation is suited to conflicts that are more serious and more active, including conflicts in which violence is present. The mediator can act as a substitute for direct contact, and as a means of communication.

There are inherent difficulties in mediation, particularly when the parties are not brought into face-to-face contact. When the mediator endeavours to represent to one party the views of the other, he tends to be identified by each party with the interests of the other. An explanation of the behaviour of the other party is treated as sympathy with that party. He soon becomes regarded by both with suspicion. Parties in conflict cannot accept neutral positions: 'if you are not with us you are against us' is a common attitude. The longer mediation continues the less, and not the more, is the mediator likely to be accepted as disinterested and unprejudiced.

(v) GOOD OFFICES

Good offices implies assistance by a third party in helping parties to examine their conflict, not as a mediator who takes part in discussions, but merely as observer or point of reference to help ensure the useful conduct of negotiations. The good offices role is even more passive than mediation. It could be limited to providing a place for meeting, or a chairman of a meeting. Where the parties will not meet, it could be merely the conveying of messages between them. It is the closest approximation to negotiation, and the farthest from judicial processes. Of all techniques it implies the least intervention in the dispute. Indeed, the role of good offices is sometimes merely to bring parties together in conditions in which an initiative by them to propose a meeting is not expedient. The power or bargaining positions of the parties are not restrained, new information is not contributed, and the relationships are in accord with direct negotiations with all the accompanying drawbacks.

In any situation there are likely to be mixtures of these pure forms, and in practice elements of each might be discerned in the one act of third party intervention. An institution such as a regional organisation or the United Nations is likely to sponsor means for the peaceful settlement of disputes that vary from judicial processes right through the spectrum to recommendations that the parties themselves should negotiate. The one dispute could be subjected to each of these techniques at different stages.

(vi) SUPPORTIVE TECHNIQUES

Supportive techniques employed within societies are even closer to direct negotiation than is good offices. There are those that are associated with casework and social work generally. The supportive approach of casework is designed to provide a structure in which the individual can adjust to the demands made upon him by the environment, and psychoanalytical methods are an extension of this. The same procedures can be adapted to the needs of group conflict: what intervention there is has the positive purpose of providing knowledge and insights that might assist the parties in the resolution of their conflict. These techniques acknowledge that resolution of conflict comes from the parties: no suggestion or persuasion by a third party is likely to help. The third party identifies with the opposing parties, perceives the relationship as they do, yet the role of the third party is an active one, helping the parties to identify the problem. [10]

(vii) CONTROLLED COMMUNICATION

It is in this perspective of traditional techniques and more recent developments that the role of controlled communication can best be perceived. Controlled communication is a further step in the same direction, away from third party decision-making and towards direct negotiation between the parties. It is at least as neutral as good offices in the sense that suggestions and recommendations are not within the role of the third party. On the other hand, the role of the third party is in this case an active one, probably as active as that of the conflicting parties. It is to inject into discussion new information, not about the dispute in question, but about conflict, its origins and processes drawn from theoretical analyses and empirical studies. Whether it takes the form of separate contact with each of the parties – as in mediation – or face-to-face communication between parties – as in negotiation – it seeks to control communication by providing the parties with insights into their own behaviour and that of their oppositions. Its prime function is to prepare the ground for negotiation by establishing the conditions in which negotiation will lead to de-escalation and avoid escalation of conflict, to extend the range of choices of functional cooperation, and generally to present the conflict as a problem to be solved and not as a contest to be won.

(viii) NEGOTIATIONS

'Negotiation' is a term differently used in different contexts. Sometimes it is a generic term used to include all non-judicial and arbitral processes, such as conciliation and mediation.[11] For reasons of clarity it is convenient to restrict the use of this term to exchanges that take place directly between the parties, that is, in the absence of third parties.

Negotiations of this direct type have an advantage over judicial processes because the whole of a relationship can be discussed, including political aspects. Furthermore, they can be held in secret. No third party suggests, influences or coerces, and the parties retain their independence of decision. Judicial processes and negotiations are two extremes: the one removes decision-making from the parties, and the other leaves it wholly with the parties.

There is no more frequently employed means of controlling relationships between states than negotiation, and probably conflict avoidance sometimes results from it. However, negotiations of this direct type have a limited place in the peaceful settlement of disputes once they occur, especially once the level of conflict has escalated. There are many reasons for this. If direct contact is possible between parties in conflict, the probability is that one will be in a position to coerce the other, and a negotiated settlement is likely to lead to an agreement which creates conflict in the future. Peace settlements are negotiated in a victor–vanquished framework, and negotiation that avoids hostilities is no less within a power framework. Even compromise settlements arrived at because the power relationship is not clear-cut, are likely to provide the origins of future conflict. There being no external source of information and experience, and no alternatives except those the parties themselves produce, the range of choice is limited. Having in mind the prejudices, images and stereotypes, suspicions and fears of parties involved in a conflict situation, the probability of further escalation of conflict during negotiation would be as high as conflict resolution.

A study of diplomacy, which is the common procedural means of negotiation, demonstrates how inadequate it proves to be in the handling of serious disputes. The practice of breaking off diplomatic relations is evidence of its inadequacy. Diplomacy can contribute to tension and create conflict situations when it is used as a tool of power politics, employing misinformation to achieve its ends, and perhaps even deliberately creating tension between other states.

In cases of serious conflict direct negotiation is usually impossible, at least until one party has demonstrated its superior power position. This limits negotiation as a process to a range of conflicts not likely to lead to the use of force, or to a stage before force is employed.

The ultimate ideal is for controlled communication to be self-controlled through the possession by the participants of the knowledge, theories and analytical tools now available to the scholar. Indeed, it is the prime objective of teaching and research to create conditions in which foreign office personnel are aware of the nature of conflict, and the means available for its resolution. In these circumstances negotiation becomes the ultimate in a sequence of measures each of which is further removed from coercion, and nearer to self-imposed resolution after alternative goals and means have been assessed reasonably in relation to costs of conflict.

(ix) FROM COERCION TO INDEPENDENCE

It is noticeable that there is a continuous weakening of the decision-making role of the third party as techniques progress from judicial settlements to good offices. The development of these weaker forms of intervention represents a historical continuum as well as a behavioural one: the League concentrated on judicial and arbitral processes, the United Nations far more on less formal ones. While it is difficult to assess relative success, at least without knowing how often various means have been offered and rejected, and whether the final outcome led to continuing stable conditions, there is some evidence that the less formal the technique the greater the range of application, and the greater the success.[12] Whether this be so or not, there is a presumption that each successive process has been introduced because of the failure of a previous one in a case similar to the one of current concern, or because existing ones were held to be inappropriate to the case being handled. It could be deduced that each successive process that was institutionalised was found to be more effective in relation to some types of conflict than previous ones.

Some international lawyers would maintain that the progression has not been because experience supported the use of less formal procedures, but because states were unwilling to accept the more formal ones that allowed third parties to influence conditions of settlement. This legal reaction begs the main question: if states are unwilling to adopt judicial and formal procedures that take decision-making away from them, then these procedures are irrelevant to the circumstances. It is of no avail to bemoan the condition of world society and blame states for the lack of success of some techniques. The intellectual difficulties experienced in considering traditional means of peaceful settlement of disputes cannot be overcome by suggesting improvements in existing practices, or by impressing upon states their moral obligation to fall in with behavioural patterns suggested by intellectuals and idealists. The reality is that both judicial procedures and the less formal processes of mediation or third party interventions are incompatible with the nature and operations of international, and indeed with many aspects of municipal society. They are a vestige of a primitive condition known as traditional society, now rejected in favour of processes that leave decision-making within the jurisdiction of those concerned, except in so far as decision making can be facilitated by the experience, advice and analytical assistance of specialists at the disposal of those taking decisions. What is called for is not just a reconsideration of existing procedures, but the development of ones that meet the theoretical requirements of social relationships.

Techniques for the resolution of conflict need to reflect the felt needs of world society and the actors within it. Procedures that postulate conflict as a zero sum game in which the gain of one party is the loss of the other, cannot lead to a decision that satisfies all parties. Judicial processes are of this kind. Arbitration and conciliation, and indeed even more informal procedures, postulate that bargains and compromises are desirable and possible, and that external pressures can help to make them acceptable. Such postulates have no support in behavioural studies, and the independent decision-making role of states in world society is more jealously defended than in most behavioural relationships. The techniques fail because their objective is settlement by third-party decision-making, or by compromises that do not fully and equitably satisfy the needs and aspirations of all parties. The objective must be agreement which avoids coercion, compromise and third-party decisions and pressures. The relevant search is for techniques that have this objective. In summary, judicial settlements divide a cake according to interpretations of past practices, mediation endeavours to arrive at compromises so that gains and losses can be shared, but what is required by world society are procedures that provide means of promoting relationships that increase the size of the cake and enable all parties to gain. If this has an idealistic ring it is because we are accustomed to zero sum thinking, to regarding states as being in a condition of continuing conflict, and not because of wishful thinking and unrealism. It is the purpose of this report, and of the companion study, to demonstrate that theories of functionalism and communications are more realistic, though seemingly idealistic, than traditional approaches based on the relative power positions of states and an absence of calculated gains through decision-making processes.

The inadequacies of coercive approaches to world order have been noted before. In 1941 a lawyer and sociologist, Niemeyer, in a book he called *Law Without Force*, reacted against the institutional and collective security approach to world order. He rejected the idea of a state as a united organisation, and of society as consisting of bodies and forces, and regarded them as being made up of coordinated and interrelated behaviour.[13] The role of international organisation, or the role of any system of law, was one that coordinated the respective functions of states—'a system which, instead of restricting states, represents the conditions under which their functional ends can best be attained'.[14] In his introductory remarks he suggests that 'political reality has become unlawful, because the existing system of international law has become unreal'.[15]

> In other words: the possibilities of the existing framework of international law are utterly exhausted. There is nothing we can hope for from a further development

of its basic ideas, nothing we can expect that has not already been suggested, tried and defeated. This book advances the thesis that, with our present conceptual equipment, we are incapable of redrafting the rules of international order so as to make them fit the changed political conditions. The very axioms of our thinking on international law are inadequate to fit the real situation. Whatever legal scheme, device, rule or prescription could be formulated within the traditional framework of international legal concepts will necessarily be in hopeless conflict with international politics, and will consequently continue to be overruled by the laws of that political reality.[16]

Niemeyer shows why collective security cannot succeed[17] and exposes the assumptions and reasons why irrelevant concepts have been retained for so long despite evidence of their irrelevance.[18] However, as he realised, exposure alone cannot destroy false notions, at least until practical alternatives can be demonstrated.

There is an interacting process between the development of world society and the development of thought about it. For example, there has been a growth in the number of states as a result of drives towards more and more control over decisions by communities in relation to their environment, towards greater and greater participation in decisions that affect them, and struggles to eliminate perceived injustices. New values have appeared, and have been transmitted by reason of technological developments in communications. World society has undergone sudden changes in both technological and political fields. Accompanying these environmental changes there have been developments in conceptual thinking that have transformed primitive man into a sophisticated person aware of rights and values, and possibilities of asserting them. These have been outlined by Deutsch in his *Nerves of Government*.[19] Under pressure of new models derived from technological advance, conceptual thinking about social organisation has changed. Balances have given place to cybernetics and self-steering devices as models, and in a matter of decades interpretations of human behaviour have altered accordingly. The result of this interaction is an ever accelerating rate of change in behaviour and thought. In few areas of social life is this more in evidence than in the study and handling of social non-conformity and conflict.

The significant direction of change in the handling of inter-state relations since the early beginnings of the state system has been from bilateral and largely coercive means to multilateral and largely self-imposed procedures. This trend is evident in its broad features. Prior to the evolution of contemporary world society, disputes among neighbouring city-states or partly integrated feudal states were settled by bilateral actions or negotiations. Later alliances, power balancing and interventions by third parties were evidence of the development of an inter-dependent system of states. Conflicts were increasingly multilateral, and multilateralism included attempts to prevent or resolve conflict by peaceful means. In this century the League Covenant represented an attempt to regulate, institutionalise and legitimise the process that had been evolving: it sought to combine the right of states to defend their interests with attempts to settle disputes peacefully, and to impose, by multilateral action, forms of coercion on any state held to be aggressive.

Alliances, power balances and other forms of collective security involved decisions and judgements as to the justice of military activity. To operate the collective security procedures of the League it was necessary to have some means of determining what was aggression. Consequently, legal approaches accompanied the development of international organisation. The League reflected the thinking of the age, and the hopes of philosophers that states would one day be subjected to the same kind of judicial processes to which individuals within states had been subjected since organised community life had begun. The judicial process was a symbol of the spirit of the age: a combination of arbitration and sanction, the latter being administered by those in positions of authority and power.

The progression from unqualified power relations to treaty relations, including the provisions for arbitration and judicial settlement of disputes, of which the League Covenant was an instance, was perceived at the time, and is still so perceived, as representing an important consciously-contrived means of promoting a peaceful international society. It is not clear that this was so in fact. In retrospect the many international treaties concluded after the Hague Convention of 1899, most of which included provisions for arbitration or judicial settlement, seem to have been merely a consolidation and formalisation of power relationships. The bargaining power of more powerful states, and the position of victor states, ensured that treaties made would be no other than agreements arrived at on a power basis, and the arbitration and judicial means of settlement of disputes no other than forms of coercion of lesser states by greater powers. The League Covenant helped to regulate and to institutionalise patterns of coercive relationships which longer-term processes were progressively destroying as communications spread. It sought to impose behaviour upon states. Furthermore, the behaviour it sought to impose was that which upheld existing structures—it did not achieve any effective means of peaceful change. The League was a

reflection of a developing philosophy that attached importance to law and order: but law and order within the
League framework were conceived as ends in themselves,
whereas in retrospect they were merely superficial or
immediate objectives or means to the satisfaction of the
needs of society. If the processes of law and order destroyed other values they were not supported. The trend of
thought and behaviour was strongly towards law and
order, but only through processes that satisfied the needs
of society, and the absence of coercion no less than the
absence of aggression was one of these.

Inevitably the League failed because states valued
their independence, and refused either to have their
interests and values determined by a judiciary or institution over which they had little or no control, or to be
bound to act against other states regardless of their
interests. It failed, not because it was too idealistic, but
because it was too conservative. The Covenant represented
an endeavour to institute and formalise coercion in
world society, and to consolidate the position of those
states that were the most powerful and strove to remain
that way. It was conceived on the premise that future law
and order in inter-state society could be based upon past
experience in municipal society. This was false for two
reasons. First, the two levels of social organisation are different. Second, coercion was even then being found, as will
later be demonstrated, to be an unsuitable instrument by
which to prevent non-conformity even in municipal
society.

The Charter of the United Nations, drafted more than
twenty years later, reflected in some degree the longer-
term trends that were operating in world society. By
contrast with the Covenant it set out to harmonise the
actions of independent states (Articles 1–4) and far more

to rest upon mediation, conciliation and other peaceful means of handling disputes. To the extent that it has failed to achieve its purposes, this has been due to endeavours that were made to retain the power position of major states. The Security Council and the International Court have not played the role intended for them, and the Assembly, which was given no powers beyond a power to recommend, has increased its status. The United Nations has failed where the League failed, and for the same reasons. As is so often the case, where there has been failure there are advocates for more of the same medicine, but few for a reconsideration of the total situation, and a search for new remedies. The academic and popular response to United Nations failures sometimes takes the form of proposals for revision to provide increased powers and forms of coercion. This is reflected in both the United States (April 1962) and Soviet Union (September 1962) draft disarmament agreements and in some scholarly works.[20] These responses arise out of a misreading of history. The reasons for the different approach at San Francisco were not reasons of political expediency: the different approach was not on the grounds that if judicial processes were not acceptable, it was more sensible or easier not to try to introduce them. The trend from imposed settlement, by power or judicial decision, to self-applied or voluntary control of behaviour and resolution of conflict, was already being reflected in the thinking of the day.

Even at San Francisco, however, the nature of the change was not fully understood, despite the experiences of war. There was a greater attention paid than ever before to non-discrimination in relations between states, reflecting a memory of pre-war Japanese complaints of economic discrimination, and enforced by the presence of non-Europeans around the committee tables. While the war had not yet ended, and areas of Asia were still occupied by the Japanese, independence and development were familiar and acceptable goals. India was an active participant. However, the kind of social and political changes which would be required within states once independence was granted, and among states, some of which were powerful and developed and some of which were undeveloped, were not then understood. At no point in the Charter was it acknowledged, for example, that feudal systems were as provocative of conflict as was colonialism, that internal revolution and revolt might well be inevitable responses to oppressive circumstances, and that outside help for rebels might be as acceptable internationally as help for governments which had little popular support. On the contrary, the opening article of the Charter was couched in the traditional terms of 'suppression of acts of aggression and other breaches of the peace', and the settlement of disputes 'in conformity with the principles of justice and international law'.

It was subsequent experience of colonial revolt and unrest that drew attention to the phenomenon of 'aggression' as a response to an environment, 'insurgency' as the counterpart of foreign intervention that was designed to support a government under internal threat, 'nationalism' as a movement against foreign influence including the influence of internal structures and institutions that persisted after independence. Because the Soviet Union identified itself with these emerging values, every social change was perceived in the context of a world struggle between existing, and predominantly Western, institutions, and those of the Soviet Union. A decade had to pass before it was understood that these social movements were indigenous, and that the states were non-aligned in the wider power struggle between the United States and the Soviet Union.

Observers began, especially in the late forties in relation to the 'Indo-China problem', to make distinctions between legitimate or legal governments, and legitimised or popularly supported ones. In one form or another the distinction now forms part of most descriptions of conflict situations. (See the companion study for a discussion of legitimacy.) Once this distinction was made there could no longer be an agreed legal norm of behaviour: the possibility of 'just' revolt had to be accepted as the possibility of 'just' war had been. Furthermore, the theoretical basis of the United Nations as an organisation of independent and sovereign states was removed unless two conditions were observed: first, non-intervention in domestic affairs, and second, recognition of whatever faction succeeded in an internal struggle. In practice neither was observed: political revolt was perceived by one power or another as evidence of foreign intervention, and therefore as a matter of international concern calling for intervention, and states were not always prepared to accord recognition to governments that professed an opposing ideology, even though they were in effective administrative control. Thus the political reality of social change and traditional policies were in conflict: attempts were made by foreign powers to impose settlements within states, whereas internal conflict could be resolved finally only by reasonably satisfying demands made by revisionists upon those in control of existing political institutions.

The sixties of this century have been transition years: the international institutions formally responsible for peace and security were ones that were based upon the assumption that coercion and deterrence were the means of control, while the recognised reality is that neither great powers nor the United Nations can settle conflicts. Intervention in support of factions tends to make them less willing to seek accommodations, and tends therefore to prolong the processes of adjustment out of which a resolution finally emerges.[21] Little by little the role of the Security Council has diminished, and the processes of integration through conflict have been allowed to run free – widespread and destructive conflict between parties being one consequence. Meanwhile, with experience, forms of mediation and peacekeeping have begun to take more into account the reality that it is only the parties involved that are in a position to resolve conflicts, and that external coercion has a counter-productive effect.

Thus the trend from diplomatic history to international institutions and to behavioural studies that we noticed in examining changes in thought in this area has been reflected in attempts to control world society. The reasons for these trends will be clearer when in later chapters we consider the assumptions on which traditional policies were based. It is desired at this point merely to hypothesise, and to record early evidence of, the existence of a trend from external coercion to self-imposed decisions in the organisation of world society. The shift from an emphasis on judicial processes to mediation and conciliation reflected in the Charter was not backtracking or an admission of defeat. It reflected experience and an increased awareness of the nature of the state and of inter-state relations. It was an acknowledgement of independence movements, evidence of resistance to hegemonial relationships, and a refusal to be bound by behavioural norms determined by great powers in a past age. It was the application to international politics of the principles and values that in the domestic field led to the democratic state, and of social reactions to conditions in backward countries where attempts were being made to ensure conformity with the requirements of unacceptable institutions by means of coercion and force.

(x) SETTLEMENT AND RESOLUTION

These developments in thought and practice make necessary a clear distinction between *settlement* and *resolution* of conflict, a distinction not required within a legal or power framework. 'Settlement' has the connotation of determination by a third party, such as a court or a greater power. It could be a compromise which parties feel they have no option but to accept. 'Resolution' is used here to imply a final solution freely acceptable to all parties, one that does not destroy any important values, one parties will not wish to repudiate in the absence of changed circumstances. A conflict is resolved, as distinct from settled, when the outcome is self-supporting, and for this to happen the new relationship must be negotiated freely by the parties themselves. The difference can be determined empirically both by observing procedures, and by follow-up which reveals the final outcome of decisions taken.

The League Covenant set out principles and procedures for the peaceful settlement of disputes, in particular arbitration, judicial settlement and enquiry by the Council. The United Nations Charter includes far-reaching procedures, especially under Chapter VI concerned with the 'Pacific Settlement of Disputes'. In general these call upon parties to settle their differences by any peaceful means available; but there is threat in the background. The Security Council has the power to recommend a settlement in the absence of agreement among the parties, and under Chapter VII to take 'Action with Respect to

Threats to the Peace, Breaches of the Peace, and Acts of Aggression'.

It will be noted that 'peaceful' or 'pacific' settlement of disputes within this institutional framework means settlement without violence. Settlement without violence ranges from freely negotiated agreement between parties, to a decision imposed upon them by others. 'Peaceful', meaning without violence, does not, therefore, mean without coercion. The settlements envisaged are those dictated by the nature of international society; within a political framework settlement of conflict is by bargaining and compromises determined by, among other factors, the relative power of the parties and their allies. Sometimes settlement takes place only after the test of relative power in warfare. Even mediation and conciliation by one state, or by a nominated person, is usually of this nature; threats, bargaining and the pressures of the international system are in the background. Hence, though the traditional concept of 'peaceful' may mean without violence, it implies that the violence of parties is merely suppressed by the coercion of others. Settlement arrived at within a political framework results, therefore, in a condition of potential instability. A shift in power relations is likely to lead to the re-emergence of the conflict.

In the same way, the settlement of political disputes by judicial procedures, also provided for both by the Covenant and the Charter, could be possible and effective only by the exercise by the Security Council of its powers under Article 94 to enforce decisions of the Court. In so far as it is effective in practice it is only by reason of the political framework in which it takes place. Judicial settlements are not based upon any mutual understanding and acceptance by the parties of the different values involved. International courts are inevitably political bodies; but this factor aside, while courts may sometimes take sociological factors into consideration, it is precedence and convention that are the stronger influences, and these reflect past political structures, and the framework of international society. Judicial settlements of political disputes are political determinations in disguise; they are settlements produced within and by the political system, thus favouring existing values and structures. As important political disputes arise out of attempts to alter the political system and to challenge its values and practices, one of the parties to a judicial settlement is likely to be left with a sense of frustration or injustice, which in due course stimulates in it further attempts to alter the system. In practice states rarely submit to international judicial procedures because they are not willing to accept decisions made by an institution that does not take fully into account their interests and values.

(xi) SUMMARY

It was argued in the previous chapter that there has been a long-term trend in the analysis of inter-state politics from broad generalisations and synoptic accounts of history to micro-studies of the behaviour of states and processes that enable the observer to come closer to the subject matter, controlled communication being an extreme position not unlike psychoanalytical means of examining human behaviour. In this chapter it has been argued that there has also been a progression in dealing with conflicts from direct authoritarian judgements and enforcement of judgements, to methods that draw out the points of view of the parties, controlled communication being an extreme position not unlike psychoanalytical means of resolving conflict between the individual and his environment. This trend has several features. Not only is there less and less decision-making by third parties, but there is also less and less new information available to the parties in conflict, until finally the point of direct negotiation is reached in which there is no third party and no new information. In these latter circumstances the conflict is as likely to escalate as to be resolved. Controlled communication injects new information, not about the particular conflict but about conflict generally, including perception, escalation, problems of communication and interpretation, assessment of values and costs and other aspects of decision-making. It is in these respects a logical extension of the progression from authoritarian decision to the passivity of good offices, yet the beginning of another continuum of third-party intervention commencing with assistance in defining the problem, supplying knowledge of relationships to the parties, and leading to practical assistance in applying principles of functional cooperation, regionalism and other aspects of integration theory.

While controlled communication can be used either for theoretical analysis or for therapy, depending upon the objectives of the user, research concerned with the analysis of conflict cannot be disassociated from the resolution of conflict. Analysis is an essential part of the process of resolution, and resolution is an essential part of the testing of theoretical propositions. Controlled communication thus provides a meeting point of analysis and resolution of conflict. It is clinical application of behavioural theories to international politics.

Analytical studies of history, simulation and content analysis, and on the practical side, mediation and conciliation, do not raise in any critical way the assumptions and hypotheses that are reflected in these trends towards micro-analysis of behaviour, and away from coercion in inducing conformity. These more traditional techniques of analysis and resolution of conflict evolved over a period of time with little examination of the reasons why they did, or of trends of which they were a part. They involved, respectively, more and more detailed analysis, and less and less coercion, but no clear departure from description and from enforcement. Controlled communication, on the other hand, is a process which rests wholly upon non-coercion. As such it brings to the fore hypotheses and assumptions that were previously being entertained, but not made explicit. It is to these that we now turn.

NOTES TO CHAPTER TEN

(1) Lall, *Modern International Negotiation.*
(2) David Davies Memorial Institute of International Studies, *Report of a Study Group on the Peaceful Settlement of International Disputes.* The members of the study group were: Sir Humphrey Waldock, Lords Strang, Devlin and Shawcross, Sir John Foster, Professors R. Y. Jennings and D. H. N. Johnson, Dr D. W. Bowett, Mr J. E. S. Fawcett, Dr F. A. Mann, Mrs Hazel Fox, Mr E. Lauterpacht and Mr J. F. McMahon.
(3) Ibid. p. 38.
(4) Ibid. p. 38.
(5) Ibid. p. 34.
(6) Ibid. p. 35.
(7) Ibid. p. 36.
(8) See companion study, ch. 5.
(9) *Peaceful Settlement of International Disputes*, p. 17.
(10) See one of the many texts now available on social casework, for example, Younghusband, *New Developments in Casework.*
(11) See Lall, *Modern International Negotiation* and Ikle, *How Nations Negotiate.*
(12) Ibid.
(13) Niemeyer, *Law Without Force*, pp. 395 ff.
(14) Ibid. p. 402.

(15) Ibid. p. 9.
(16) Ibid. pp. 17–18.
(17) Ibid. p. 399.
(18) Ibid. pp. 390–1.
(19) Deutsch, *Nerves of Government.*
(20) Clark and Sohn, *World Peace Through World Law.*
(21) See companion study, ch. 3.

11 The Philosophical Basis of Settlement

In the present phase of the study of International Relations, underlying assumptions that have conditioned thought over the years are being brought to the surface, and the logical development of thought based on these assumptions examined and tested where possible. One major assumption has been that there are influences inherent in world society that induce conflict between states. The view that world society is in a condition of potential war, and is likely to remain so for all practical purposes, is widely held, especially by practitioners. Though not always stated explicitly, it is one that seems to be implied in the writings of contemporary political scientists of the historical and 'political realist' schools. It is one that seems to accord with experience. National defences, alliances, power balances and collective security arrangements are among the devices that have been designed to create some measure of stability, and to limit violence, in this assumed condition of potential war.

While there is empirical evidence of conflict of interests among and between systems and states, there is some reason for thinking that the devices designed to prevent war tend to contribute to it.[1] There is also the empirical fact that not all conflict leads to violence and war. Furthermore, even though it could be demonstrated that world society is in a potential state of war and always had been, it would not necessarily follow that world society must remain in this condition. Indeed, it has been argued[2] that a condition of 'anarchy' is one associated with every society before it evolves into a community in which common values are shared, and in which the rule of law is observed without obvious coercion, and because of shared values.

There are many variables involved, including behavioural responses to the assumption that conflicts of interest are inevitable and inevitably lead to violence in some yet unknown circumstances. That conflicts of interest exist is not in serious doubt; that these conflicts would necessarily lead to violence more frequently in the absence of control devices such as national defences and alliances, or that violence could not be avoided by appropriate decision-making processes, has not been demonstrated.

An extension of the view that violent conflict is inherent in world society, and one which judging by practice is no less widely accepted, is that conflicts can be controlled and settled within a threat framework, such as guarantees by third parties, but not resolved. In this view, the best that can be sought is no more than containment of violence. It is this extended reasoning that justifies great power interventions, the Security Council, and alliances with which are associated tacitly agreed spheres of influences in which conflict can be contained by hegemonial powers.

Those who have based their thinking upon such assumptions regarding the nature of world society, and the consequent need for control devices within which conflicts can be settled and sometimes prevented, have usually been aware of the way in which political change creates pressures upon these devices. The assumed need for control devices, which tend to support existing structures without providing for effective means of peaceful change, and the evident need for means of dealing with change, have presented philosophers and political scientists in all times with a major dilemma. Stability and change seem to be incompatible. Dialectic philosophies are different from other traditional approaches only in that they accept more explicitly the existence of a condition of conflict, and more explicitly assume that this condition must lead to an altered relationship which itself will be a condition of conflict. They seem to make virtue out of perceived necessity, as do contemporary sociologists who attribute a functional value to conflict.

The practical problem posed by these assumed conditions of world society is how to bring forces of revision and reaction into a relationship that enables peaceful change, and thus avoids the need to keep them separate, or to suppress one or the other. It was for this reason that the League and the United Nations were conceived: they sought to combine deterrence and means of change. However, an institution, even when it includes techniques of arbitration, conciliation and mediation, can contribute little to resolving the dilemma: the institution is likely to cease to be effective before such major change can be accommodated through it. If world society is in a condition of potential war, if violence can be avoided only by deterrence, it would seem to follow that an institution at which parties meet and are subjected to world pressures cannot in itself contribute to peaceful change. On the contrary, it could as readily help to escalate conflict by reason of alignments behind each of the parties.

Even though the assumptions and reasoning which led to the establishment of international collective security institutions were sound, the notion of such an institution has its own internal contradictions. In so far as an institution is to provide an effective means of deterrence and coercion within a collective security framework, the notion is in accord with the basic assumption that world society is in a condition of war in which conflicts of interest can only be settled – not resolved – and in which agreements must be enforced and policed. In so far as an institution is to provide a meeting point, and an opportunity for parties in conflict to influence one another and be influenced by a world consensus, the notion is in accord with a quite different assumption, namely, that conflicts of interest may be resolved by the parties themselves by reappraisal of gain and losses, reassessment of values currently held, shifts in values, and reperceptions of situations and attitudes. The existence of the first assumption makes difficult the acceptance of the proposition that differences of interest may be subjective and therefore alterable. The existence of the second assumption leads to doubts about the wisdom and justice of enforcing agreements and patterns of behaviour upon parties, and destroys the effectiveness of international collective security institutions.

The technique of controlled communication is a direct challenge to the assumption that international society is always in a condition of conflict because of irreconcilable differences in interests among states. The hypothesis is that conflict, like all relationships, is a subjective condition capable of alteration, and that avoidance and resolution of conflict are possible by wholly non-coercive means. It suggests by means of empirical investigation that there are alternatives to settlements traditionally arrived at by the intervention of other powers, by threat, or by third-party guarantees.

It could reasonably be argued that controlled communication avoids the traditional dilemma of stability or change merely by paying no attention to the irreconcilable interests that exist in world society, and by confining attention to the types of manipulative interests and values that are known to exist among persons and groups in developed communities. But the hypothesis is not that there exists in world society a community relationship in which there are widely shared values that determine behaviour and which can be manipulated. The hypothesis is that conflicts of interest are not different in community and society relationships, but that in a society relationship, because it is a society relationship, and because issues of national importance are involved, procedures of resolution are required that bring to the surface cost and advantage and alternative goals, more effectively than is usually required in relationships within a community. Stated another way, the traditional view is that a society relationship such as exists between states requires control by power and coercion exercised by some international authority because it lacks community values. Controlled communication seeks to test the hypothesis that there is no difference between society and community relationships, except those of communication, language and ethnic differences and far from requiring more coercive procedures, conformity with a consensus in world society can be promoted most effectively by even less coercion than is thought necessary in communities, and by more opportunities for overcoming communications problems and for making accurate cost-advantage calculations.

Before examining more closely the assumptions of controlled communication, which is done in the next chapter, it will be helpful first to obtain a perspective on more traditional attitudes and why they persist.

(i) THE LEGAL APPROACH

The legal structure of law enforcement was in early municipal society the embodiment of the assumption of the existence of a persistent condition of irreconcilable differences of interests and of potential conflict. Sometimes the conflict was perceived as being between feudal lords and peasants, or between society and vagabonds. With social change, with alterations in values and growth in community relations, law-making and law enforcement became less authoritarian, less arbitrary, and far more a reserve control than part of a coercive social structure. Public hearings, the jury and appeal systems reflected these changes. What was once a coercive role is, in the contemporary society, more and more becoming a sympathetic one with the goal of facilitating the adjustment of the individual to his environment, and of individuals and groups to each other. It is now being realised that the nature of non-conformity was previously misconceived. Vagabonds were not just lazy people: they were products of a system that made no provision for unemployment caused by industrial change. Delinquents are now more and more found to be persons on whom the environment imposes demands too heavy for many to bear. The judicial role of the court is found to be less and less appropriate for cases coming before it, and sometimes what was thought to be a judicial function is now being carried out by the social worker at the request of the court.

It is to be noted that while significant changes have taken place over decades in social and economic structures it is not these changes that have altered attitudes to and the handling of non-conformity. There have not been significant structural changes in municipal society since capital punishment was in force, and since homosexuality was regarded as a criminal offence. The comparison is not between society and community behaviour, it is between approaches to behaviour whether in a society or a community relationship.

So also in world society: there is no reason to assume that coercion is any more relevant in the relations of states in the world society than it was thought to be necessary in the relations of groups in the municipal environment. On the contrary, in the light of the universality of patterns of behaviour to which General Systems Theory draws attention, there is reason to expect scientific discovery in relation to municipal systems to apply to any social system, societal or communal, municipal or international.

There is still a widespread belief among international lawyers that world society requires, and could conceivably develop, a rule of law not unlike the authoritative laws of traditional societies. While there are many schools of thought on the nature and organs of international law, there seems to be a general agreement on the desirability, and indeed the practicability in due course of:

(a) a set of normative rules for the guidance of states and other international actors in their relations with each other, and especially to restrain aggression, violence and conflict;

(b) some form of third party to recommend action, to interpret law, or otherwise to bring to bear the views and values of other members of the world society; and

(c) some form of sanction to enforce law, the decisions of international agents, or the clearly expressed will of world society.

Evidence of this belief is plentiful. Brierly has observed:

No lawyer is likely to doubt the desirability of a much greater readiness on the part of states than they at present show to accept the settlement of their disputes on the basis of law. The present unlimited freedom of states to reject that method of settlement is entirely indefensible; it makes possible the grossest injustices, and it is a standing danger to the people of the world by encouraging the habit of states to regard themselves each as a law unto itself.[3]

Brierly may not be representative of contemporary international lawyers, but he reflects a generally acceptable legal approach to international relations. Friedmann is less traditional, but he agrees that,

> There is a burning and vital need for the establishment of effective international military force, as provided for in the hitherto abortive provisions of the UN Charter, a force that will be able to enforce the authority of the international community against all states, big and small. There is a need for the extension of the jurisdiction of the International Court of Justice, and for enforcement powers that will make defiance of its judgments . . . impossible.[4]

Jenks holds the same view. In his view the primary functions which law must fulfil include debarring recourse to armed force, save in the common interest, and mutual aid to restrain acts of aggression, both of which imply an ability to determine when the use of force is in the common interest, and what is aggression.[5]

International lawyers have recently been influenced, as have been political scientists, by sociological thinking, and are endeavouring to include within traditional legal frameworks an acknowledgement of behavioural responses. Some postulate the duty of courts to take account of these, and be decision-makers in respect of them. They believe that attempts should be made to broaden the more straightforward legal approach, and to take into account different perceptions of aggressiveness, defence, intervention and self-determination that parties have in different circumstances, and to reflect sociological thinking in 'positive decision-making' by courts.[6]

At first sight this is an encouraging development, and an attempt to break away from personal interpretations of normative rules derived from past practices of powerful states responding to past environments, which clearly provide no satisfactory or generally acceptable basis for determining the behaviour of states, old and new, in the contemporary world. But looked at more closely this behavioural approach to international law is reactionary in two ways. First, it is a regression into an authoritarian framework, in which courts determine values and normative rules of behaviour. True, the intention is that judges should be in a position to declare their personal values instead of making on legal grounds judgements which reflect prejudice. True, also, that the intention is that this should be done in a more enlightened way, taking into account what knowledge is available to social scientists. However, except in so far as it is intended to apply positive decision-making only to parties that submit voluntarily to the jurisdiction of courts, what is being suggested is the type of authoritarian decision-making that has been associated with traditional societies. It is not for courts to determine values, and perhaps not even when the parties concerned agree that they should do so, for thereby precedents are established that could affect others. In so far as international lawyers do intend that this form of decision-making should be limited to parties that voluntarily submit their disputes to them, they are likely to be concerned with a small number of unimportant cases not in any event likely to lead to violence, and the approach therefore is of no special value or significance.

This approach is reactionary in a second sense. The tendency is for non-judicial institutions gradually to assume functions previously carried out by courts, and to act in ways designed to assist the parties themselves in finding a resolution of their conflict. Positive decision-making by courts shares the approach of traditional law in a traditional society, in which it is assumed that settlements can only be imposed, and that resolution of conflict is not possible. They have not broken away from the widely held view that states must submit to third-party decisions.

Traditional law has had a measure of legitimised status: there is a consensus that admits to the relevance of past cases and a developing common law, safeguarded frequently by appeal systems that finally draw the attention of the legislature to injustices within the law. But this so-called behavioural approach to international law seems wholly to deny the demands of legitimisation: authority is assumed, and not derived from legislation or past practices. Courts have always reflected prejudices: under this procedure prejudice would be institutionalised. The making of value judgements and arbitrary decisions would be a right and a duty – just the elements that modern society has persistently struggled to eliminate from judicial processes.

One justification of this conservative approach is that developments in municipal society are not necessarily relevant to international society: in the one case there are community relations controlled by community consensus, and in the other disorganised social relationships that require authoritarian control in the absence of community consensus. But the original justification for a legal approach to international order was that what is done in municipal society should be done in world society – as quotations above show. Either the analogy is relevant or it is not. In municipal society it is now recognised that coercion has not been an effective means of avoiding deviant behaviour. Why not apply with some consistency experience in municipal society to international society?

Positive law-making, which takes non-legal argument into account, is, in effect, arbitration. As already observed, it is far from clear how arbitration decisions are made, why some influences and not others are taken into account. This merely increases the arbitrary nature of law-making which is already a reason why judicial processes are not usually acceptable in world society.

One reason for this blockage in thought among international lawyers is that there is a strong prejudice against violence as such, and the prevention of violence is regarded in itself as a social goal to be achieved. Repression of violence by threatened violence is acceptable, but not violence. This is implicit in the United Nations Charter, and Jenks has spelt it out.

> The obligation of members to refrain in their international relations from the threat or use of force in any manner inconsistent with the purposes of the United Nations is absolute. Without such an obligation the prospect of maintaining world peace by more effective international organisation becomes altogether illusory. No ideological qualification of the obligation can be regarded as acceptable. Any attempt to import such a qualification into the obligation will inevitably so destroy the obligation itself as to defeat the purposes of those who seek to qualify it. The concept that the obligation cannot be invoked to restrain those chafing against injustice by the continuing aggression of a colonial, post-colonial or neo-colonial régime not only mis-states the problem; it makes both the problem of peace and the problem of justice wholly impossible of solution. The obligation becomes meaningless and inoperative if we allow it to be qualified by anything other than the necessary right of individual and collective self-defence, reasonably construed and subject to impartial review.[7]

This is a traditional view: it fails to differentiate

between violence and coercion designed to prevent change and reaction to this violence and coercion associated with a desire for change. It is this which renders law conservative, and a disruptive force in society over a period of time when frustrated change finally gives rise to violence that no system of law and order can contain. Even the conservative Roman Catholic Church has a doctrine of persistent injustice by which violence can be justified. As will be argued in the next chapter, it is not sufficient to treat all conflict and violence as a single phenomenon: there are different types of conflict, and each requires different treatment if violence is to be avoided. Certainly it is not consistent to regard the use of force as immoral or unlawful when it is designed to promote change, but lawful and moral when it is employed to prevent it. The use of power and of violence are behavioural responses to an environment either by factions seeking change or seeking to prevent it, and neither behaviour is more or less moral than the other.

Another reason for a mental blockage is a more practical one. If conformity cannot be guaranteed by legal judgements and enforcement, and must be brought about by a process of interaction between parties, then the role of law and lawyers is no longer relevant outside the narrow one of interpretation of documents and agreements. The introduction of behavioural considerations as a source of law has the effect, logically, of eliminating law because behavioural considerations lead to processes of assisted self-determinations of the type made possible within a controlled communications framework. The so-called legal function contemplated by lawyers who advocate positive decision-making would be better carried out by sociologists and in the absence of the rigidities of legal convention and procedures.

The adherence to third-party judgement is persistent. To refer again to Jenks, 'There can be no peace without the renunciation of war, the acceptance of third-party judgement, . . .'.[8] Yet both a behavioural analysis and experience of judicial or quasi-judicial procedures strongly suggest that third-party judgements and enforcing of judgements are irrelevant to the nature of the international system, and indeed of all social systems in which participation in decision-making is a value highly rated. To have them accepted by political, moral or any other pressure is likely to result in future conflict, for the settlements arrived at will not be those that are acceptable to the parties. Not all lawyers cling to third-party procedures. Stone argued 'If . . . we tried to clamp the "rule of law" on states by requiring every dispute to be settled by binding decisions of an international court this would freeze vested rights as they now are and make it even more difficult to adjust legal rights to rapidly changing conditions. There is obviously not the slightest hope that states will agree to this.'[9] He goes further and suggests that programmes for establishment of the rule of law could do harm. They conceal the basic problems. 'The refusal by states to accept third-party judgement over the wide range of such conflicts which most threaten international peace is a stark act of international life. And no hopes for a rule of law, however eloquently expressed, are likely to make it disappear.'[10]

(ii) THE MILITARY APPROACH

A second assumption behind the notion of settlement, and which arises out of the assumption that only settlements are possible, is that the handling of conflicts within and among smaller states is an obligation of greater powers. This is probably a carry-over from the days of power balances, and a condition in which control of world society was in the hands of a few larger European states. Even when the spill-over effect involves one of the greater powers as a belligerent party, as was the case in Vietnam, the generally held assumption is that the super-states can effectively control the behaviour of smaller ones. In the problem of Cyprus there was activity by Greece and Turkey because they believed that they had some direct rights and interests, and by Britain and the United States. So also in relation to the Middle East conflict of 1967, all the greater states endeavoured to exercise an influence.

Where there is a failure at the United Nations to settle a conflict, the reason that is most frequently offered is that there has not been agreement among the greater powers. This diverts attention from the far more fundamental question: can greater states, even when in agreement, impose their wills successfully upon others? The question broadly phrased in this way applies to cases in which the two super-powers are involved in relation to smaller states (Israel and Arab States), cases in which the super-powers are involved in relation to another great power (China), and also cases in which smaller states endeavour to determine the behaviour of an even smaller state (Greece and Turkey in relation to Cyprus). This question is of both academic and practical importance because it touches upon the nature of world politics, in addition to the more specific problems of international organisation and the resolution of conflict.

There are several separate questions implied in the general one posed above. Is the international system such that greater powers have power or influence over smaller states even in the absence of deliberate policies; does the mere existence of greater powers, and do the decisions they take unilaterally in their day-to-day domestic and foreign activities, determine the behaviour of smaller states? States respond to their environment by adjusting to it, by endeavouring to isolate themselves from some of its influences, or by attempting to alter it. Smaller states have little option but to react to an economic and political environment that is greatly influenced by invention, innovation, capital accumulation, ideas and other changes that tend to originate in the larger and more developed states. In this sense greater states, and the super-powers in particular, tend to determine the world environment and the behaviour of smaller states within it. In their strategic policies smaller states are especially influenced by the behaviour of greater states. Western governments that rely upon the United States for their security – and the same can probably be said of Eastern European governments that rely upon the Soviet Union – do not have to be instructed as to their domestic and foreign policies. They perceive their freedom of choice as being between survival under United States protection or being insecure without it. The United States did not instruct Australia to send troops to Korea and Vietnam.

Do greater powers consciously endeavour to impose their wills upon smaller states? Clearly there are both subtle and blatant forms of coercion. One can recall to mind many cases of economic persuasion and of direct military intervention by a greater power to prevent or to bring about social and political change in a smaller state.

It could be deduced from these two questions and answers that greater states either attract conformity to their policies, or endeavour to impose their policies when this is necessary. The first question relates to cases in which a smaller state assesses its interests and values in such a way as to lead it to accept the hegemony of larger states. In these cases, however, smaller states have a motive: it is strategic support. It could as readily be argued that the super-state is in the power of smaller states. Australia sent troops to Korea and Vietnam to obligate the United States in its defence. The United States was trapped into supporting the *de facto* government at Saigon, and was unable to exercise its freedom to pursue what later appeared to many of its decision-makers to be its national interests. This happened to be a conspicuous case; but less conspicuously it was not an unusual situation, as the British government knows as a result of its endeavours to free itself from obligations in Singapore.

The second question is concerned with special cases in which smaller states are politically (in terms of traditions, values and institutions), economically or geographically within the sphere of a larger state and can be coerced by it. But the argument that the more powerful state can determine their policies is double-edged. The implication of coercion is that the smaller states are continually struggling to gain freedom to alter their social and political institutions and policies. The fact that the United States attempted to coerce Guatemala, Cuba and the Dominican Republic is evidence, not of super-state pre-eminence, but of an unprecedented challenge to a super-state by some of the smallest states placed squarely in the geographical and economic sphere of interest of a super-state.

Thus we are led to consider a third question, can a super-state effectively attract conformity or impose its will upon a smaller one? By 'effectively' is meant continuously and without political and economic costs that are greater than the value of the gains to the super-state. Think upon Greece, Egypt, Vietnam, Congo, Korea and

Germany; Yugoslavia, Hungary, Rumania, Poland and Albania; and Aden, Cyprus, Singapore and Rhodesia.

The hypothesis that greater states are in a position to control conflicts within and among smaller states reflects a misreading of history. Whatever might have been the position in past centuries, this century has been characterised by a challenge to non-legitimised power at all domestic and inter-state levels. The prominent position of great powers in world affairs has been due to their defensive responses, not to their pre-eminence. This is as true of the Soviet Union in Eastern Europe as it is of the United States in its spheres of influence. The Middle East Crisis of 1967 supplied evidence of this. The full details of negotiations that preceded war will probably remain unknown. It appears from the speech delivered by President Nasser on 23 July 1967 that he refrained from taking the advice of his generals, who feared a pre-emptive strike by Israel, because of his belief that the United States would intervene to defend Israel. Apparently France promised to take the side of the party that did not commence hostilities and the Soviet Union warned Israel against pre-emptive action. Some attempts appear to have been made to persuade both sides to negotiate though we do not know whether or not this was a tactic to mislead the United Arab Republic as has been suggested by the Arabs. Pressures not to commence hostilities and to negotiate seem to have been ignored by one or other party. Whatever were the demands of the great powers, it does appear that they were not carried into effect. Certainly the outcome was not of the choosing of the great powers, and this alone seems to deny the validity of the proposition that they can control or determine the behaviour of other states. They intervened and meddled; but their purposes were not achieved. So, too, in the case of Cyprus, Greece and Turkey, with the United States in the background, tried to determine the future of Cyprus. The two communities in Cyprus were restrained in their own endeavours to reach an agreement. But the final outcome was not the one determined by Greece, Turkey or any great power.

It is not only super-states that have lost their power but any instrument that endeavours to coerce. If a United Nations Charter were to be drafted today one would anticipate even less emphasis upon coercion and international forces and even greater attention given to the avoidance of conditions that lead to conflict. The cause of conflict would be seen as a response of states to their environment, including other states, and the means of avoidance would be attempts to alter the environment, to alter the perception by states of their environment, and to help them in their adjustment problems. It would be a Charter that paid even less respect to military and economic powers, and by implication, to traditional and municipal concepts of law.

In short, coercion, either by greater powers or by supranational institutions, has a declining relevance for world society. It is employed, and will continue to be employed, with undesired and unintended results by states that are ill-equipped in relevantly trained and experienced politicians and officials; it will cause reactions and conflicts, and it will delay social and political change and development at least until more learning experiences like Vietnam have occurred. In the meantime smaller states are learning to avoid the intervention of great powers, and neutralism and regional settlement of disputes are evidence of this. Nonalignment is a practical means of avoiding some of the opportunities super-states otherwise have to meddle ineffectively in the affairs of other states. Even super-states will find non-intervention in the affairs of other states and freedom from alliances to be a convenient policy after more experience in contemporary world politics.

So far it has been argued that super-states and international organisations cannot effectively coerce even though they have the military and economic power to interfere in the affairs of other states. However, it is not clear that in practice they have this power. Not only does resistance to coercion or the value attached to independence make coercion costly, but competitive demands by the welfare state reduce the available wherewithal. The modern super-state is no longer one in which a ruling élite can monopolise resources for its own foreign purposes. There are competing demands on resources in the welfare state which act as a restraint on even the greatest of super-states in its endeavours to coerce the peoples of a small and underdeveloped country. A super-state in a position of pre-eminence requires a capacity to coerce many states at once: it has no pre-eminence if it must hesitate to be involved in more than one extensive conflict at a time for fear of costs and internal social revolt. Furthermore, the modern super-state is restrained by the consensus of world society, and above all, of its own society. If there happens to be a national sentiment within the super-state that recognises the right of other peoples to be independent, that acknowledges the need for national self-respect, that supports social and political reform, that sees no value or virtue in a state performing a world police role against the wishes of many other states, then the political leaders of such a super-state will either find themselves out of office, or be forced to divert military resources to coerce their own people.

The argument that greater powers determine world

order fails, apart from these reasons, because of one development in world society that is peculiar to the twentieth century, and from which there is no turning back. World society is no longer an organisation of states: it is a complex of systems that cut across state boundaries. The typical United States based world-wide industrial company has interests that are not necessarily those of a government at Washington. It has production processes distributed among many states, and it relies upon stable political peaceful conditions within them. Social reform, and popularly led governments such as have been opposed by Western powers under United States leadership, are acceptable to international business. It finds ways of treating with communist countries, even those that are not recognised by its government. Similarly, the commercial systems based in the Soviet Union extend throughout the world, even to the extent of having an interest in private wholesale trade in capitalist countries. Modern technology, specialisation, markets and communications are rendering state boundaries less and less of a restraint on transactions, and in so doing makes differences in the size and power of states less and less relevant to world society.

(iii) THE 'POLITICAL REALIST' APPROACH

In the background of both legal and military approaches is that of the political realist, the person who adopts history and experience, and personal judgements about the moral and educational limits of men, as empirical evidence. There are few better exponents than Reinhold Niebuhr.

> The fact that the coercive factor in society is both necessary and dangerous seriously complicates the whole task of securing both peace and justice. History is a long tale of abortive efforts toward the desired end

of social cohesion and justice in which failure was usually due either to the effort to eliminate the factor of force entirely or to an undue reliance upon it. Complete reliance upon it means that new tyrants usurp the places of eminence from which more traditional monarchs are cast down. Tolstoian pacifists and other advocates of non-resistance, noting the evils which force introduces into society, give themselves to the vain illusion that it can be completely eliminated, and society organised upon the basis of anarchistic principles. Their conviction is an illusion, because there are definite limits of moral goodwill and social intelligence beyond which even the most vital religion and the most astute educational programme will not carry a social group, whatever may be possible for individuals in an intimate society. The problem which society faces is clearly one of reducing force by increasing the factors which make for a moral and rational adjustment of life to life; of bringing such force as is still necessary under responsibility of the whole of society; of destroying the kind of power which cannot be made socially responsible. . .; and of bringing forces of moral self-restraint to bear upon types of power which can never be brought completely under social control. Every one of these methods has its definite limitations. Society will probably never be sufficiently intelligent to bring all power under its control. The stupidity of the average man will permit the oligarch, whether economic or political, to hide his real purposes from the scrutiny of his fellows and to withdraw his activities from effective control. Since it is impossible to count on enough moral goodwill among those who possess irresponsible power to sacrifice it for the good of the whole, it must be destroyed by coercive methods and these will always run the peril of introducing new forms of injustice in place of those abolished. . . .

The future peace and justice of society therefore depend upon, not one but many, social strategies, in all of which moral and coercive factors are compounded in varying degrees. So difficult is it to avoid the Scylla of despotism and the Charybdis of anarchy that it is safe to hazard the prophecy that the dream of perpetual peace and brotherhood for human society is one which will never be fully realised. It is a vision prompted by the conscience and insight of individual man, but incapable of fulfilment by collective man. It is like all true religious visions, possible of approximation but not of realisation in actual history.

And regarding institutional forms of peacekeeping,

The balance-of-power system may, despite its defects, become the actual consequence of present policies. The peace of the world may be maintained perilously and tentatively, for some decades, by an uneasy equilibrium between the . . . great powers. . . .

While a balance between the great powers may be the actual consequence of present policies, it is quite easy to foreshadow the doom of such a system. No participant in a balance is ever quite satisfied with its own position. Every center of power will seek to improve its position: and every such effort will be regarded by the others as an attempt to disturb the equilibrium. There is sufficient mistrust between the great nations, even while they are still locked in the intimate embrace of a great common effort, to make it quite certain that a mere equilibrium between them will not suffice to preserve the peace.

Thus a purely realistic approach to the problem of world community offers as little hope of escape from anarchy as a purely idealistic one.[11]

No scholar of the nuclear age is likely to rest content with these observations – at least in the absence of far more empirical testing of assertions about the nature of men, and the impossibility of devising institutions that fulfil social needs more effectively.

NOTES TO CHAPTER ELEVEN

(1) See Burton, *Peace Theory*.
(2) See Schwarzenberger, *Power Politics*.

(3) Brierly, *The Law of Nations*, p. 368.
(4) Friedmann, *The Changing Structure of International Law*, p. 94.
(5) Jenks, *Law in the World Community*, pp. 57–8.
(6) See Higgins, 'Policy Considerations and the International Judicial Process', pp. 58–84.
(7) Jenks, *Law in the World Community*, p. 58.
(8) Ibid. p. 35.
(9) Stone, *Law and Policy in the Quest for Survival*, p. 7.
(10) Ibid. p. 10.
(11) Quoted from Atwater, Forster and Prybyla, *World Tensions: Conflict and Accommodation*, pp. 103–6.

12 The Philosophical Basis of Resolution

Differences in viewpoints on the control of behaviour, and especially whether conflicts must be settled by external decision and collective security coercion, or can be resolved by assisted decision-making by the parties involved, arise out of different notions on the nature of behaviour. If the behaviour being examined were believed to be in the nature of reflex actions, or a reaction to a stimulus according to a biologically determined pattern, there would be good grounds for postulating that some physical restraints would be required for its control, or at least a long process of conditioning in the absence of external control. Certain types of dogs have an inbred tendency to chase and kill cats and rabbits, and cannot easily be trained not to do so, and must be restrained. If, on the other hand, the behaviour being examined were believed to be a reaction to perceived but non-existent threat, then there would be good grounds for postulating that control could be exercised by injecting knowledge and experience into relationships. A sheep farmer handling large numbers of lambing ewes takes out his dog and walks around the sheep with the dog at heel well before lambing so that the dog will not be perceived as a threat any more than is the farmer, but can nevertheless be used when required to cut out a sheep needing attention.

Fights between people occur once threat is perceived. Sometimes the threat is perceived but not existing, sometimes it is real: in the latter case containment of the threat by a third party might be appropriate, but it would promote a sense of injustice and aggressive behaviour in the former case.

There are great difficulties in determining the nature of behaviour, not merely because of difficulties in determining the empirical issues that are involved. Even if all the details of a situation were to be known, which never is the case, there would still be the problem of determining whether and at what precise stages one stimulus merges into another. An innocent party, perceived to be a threat and so accused suffers a sense of injustice, and if restrained by a third party because of the alleged threat, becomes aggressive. (This could plausibly be put forward as an explanation of China's behaviour after its revolution.) Aggressive behaviour could continue after restraints were removed, or even acquire additional and secondary motivations while the restraints were being exercised, thus translating a sense of injustice into a totally new situation. Injustice, frustration, aggression, arrogance and cruelty are all interrelated conditions, and it is not always possible to describe one without reference to the others. Child behaviour is described by reference to stimulus and environmental conditions, sometimes delinquency is also seen from the point of view of the delinquent, more rarely is this so with group behaviour. State behaviour, which always has a history which would lend itself to such an analysis, is not usually described or explained in terms of behavioural responses to an environment. History records states that were 'aggressive' and others that took 'defensive' action. Little attempt is made to explain relationships in terms that would reveal whether the state taking the defensive action had previously been imposing a perceived injustice upon the state that finally became an aggressor, or whether, to give another possibility, there was a third party creating conditions of frustration and injustice which caused the one state to strike out against the other as a scapegoat.

(i) BEHAVIOUR AS A RELEVANT RESPONSE

A first assumption implicit in the technique of controlled communication is that the behaviour of communities and states is a response to the environment, and if this behaviour includes 'aggression' then it is because this appears to the subject, in the light of the information available about the perceived environment, to be the appropriate, most beneficial response. If we were prepared to analyse community and state behaviour as part of general systems behaviour, this would not be an assumption, it would be axiomatic. Systems respond to their environment, and the presumption is that the response is for the system a predetermined one, which if relevant to the circumstances will help to preserve the system and if irrelevant will help to destroy it. In this sense the assumption stated above does not necessarily reflect a belief, an ideology, or a theory of behaviour outside that which can be deduced from General Systems Theory.

This observation can be stated in terms of change. A system in reacting to its environment can adapt itself, or alternatively when this is inconvenient or not possible, it can seek to change the environment.[1] As has been suggested, there are some distinctive differences between violence which is spontaneous, and that which is deliberately employed in legitimised and institutionalised forms as a means of access to decision-making or as a means of promoting change.

It follows from this assumption that when communities and states act aggressively, implying a behaviour that is likely to be costly in physical or social terms to themselves as well as to others, they are doing so because of some perceived threat to their interests and values. For this reason a settlement of conflict (as distinct from a resolution of conflict) would require enforcement. The perceived injustice or threat would not be removed by a legal decision, or by military defeat and an enforced undertaking to accept a particular settlement. A peace settlement is likely to increase rather than to decrease a sense of injustice and threat, especially if territories are removed, and ethnic groups taken away from the state alleged to be aggressive, and finally defeated in war. Nor is perceived injustice or threat removed by supervision or separation of parties, as when a third party intervenes before there is a victor–vanquished relationship, and determines the basis of settlement in a conflict. In this case the settlement is likely to be perceived as unjust by all parties concerned because it is likely to involve compromises. Such a settlement cannot be stable.

A corollary to the above is that responses to the environment are or are not relevant depending upon whether or not they provide an effective means of adjusting either the system to the environment or the environment to the system. Up to the present the terms 'reaction' and 'response' have been used interchangeably, but there is a useful distinction to be made between the two. 'Reaction' refers to the simple reflex or immediate behaviour following upon a stimulus, and 'response' to the experienced or reasoned behaviour that takes into account likely reactions and responses of behaviour. When A threatens or damages B, B could react by immediate retaliation, and only a third party could prevent conflict until one or other party withdrew. If, on the other hand, B responded by taking into account the probable escalation consequences of his behaviour, escalated conflict might be avoided. Similarly, A could have responded to whatever stimulus originally provoked his behaviour in ways that might have avoided his aggression against B. A clear-cut example of the difference between reaction and response is in behaviour that is directed against a scapegoat, and reasoned behaviour that avoids aggression against an object even though at first sight it might appear to have been the origin of the stimulus.

A high proportion of total behaviour is as unreasoned, unthinking or unlearned as is perception. 'It is common to hear people in everyday conversation making such remarks as "thinking this thing through". These comments seem to underline the fact that whenever possible we seem to avoid thinking, if by thinking is meant the breaking out into new ways of organizing our stored information in dealing with new situations.'[2] It has been argued that thinking is no different from the acquisition of a skill.[3] As with a skill some persons have a greater aptitude than others and it can be developed. It is a skill which experience with controlled communication suggests is widely possessed by decision-makers and their advisers in the fields of foreign policy. From this it can be deduced that assistance given to parties in conflict to help them perceive and reason about their responses could help to render responses more relevant, less costly, and probably, therefore, less aggressive. Settlement, on the other hand, can contribute nothing to perception or learning, except perhaps to reinforce perceived injustice and the need for aggressive responses.

(ii) THE SUBJECTIVE NATURE OF CONFLICT

Underlying these observations regarding behaviour there is an implication that all conflict is subjective: if controlled communication can help to avoid or to resolve conflict there must be alternative responses that can satisfy the needs of the parties.

There are two aspects in which conflicts of interest are subjective. At a given moment of time there can be differences of interest between parties that may be termed 'objective' differences in the sense that they are irreconcilable, as when two parties seek the same territory or position. But it is axiomatic that differences of interest are subjective when values are taken into account. No goal or value is absolute: there is a limit to which a party will go in sacrificing other goals in order to attain a particular one. Other values have to be preserved: there is a costing process which is a subjective one. Controlled communication is a means by which competing values are brought to attention, and alternative goals and alternative means of achieving goals, are discovered. Indonesia and Malaysia were fighting from 1964 to 1966 on a common border. Both were experiencing internal problems, and seemed to welcome the apparent external threat as a means towards internal integration. More productive means of achieving their ends required cooperation between them, planning and other time-consuming negotiations at a period when negotiation was not easy. Once costs of attaining goals in terms of loss of other goals, and alternative means of attaining goals, were considered by each party, and means were explored of attaining common goals so that both sides gained, the subjective nature of conflict became apparent.

A second feature of conflicts of interests that makes

them subjective is the perception of the parties. This is dealt with in the companion study where it is argued that conflict is not due to the natural aggressiveness or the expansionist nature of states, but to problems of communication and perception, and to escalation resulting from these. In many conflicts, origins are pushed into the background, and because of changed conditions are no longer relevant; but the conflict can persist in relation only to its escalated effects, rendering the conflict wholly subjective in character.

So far we have been concerned with parties in conflict in given environmental conditions, and have concentrated upon their values and perceptions. In reality parties frequently become involved in violent conflict in the first place because of the environment, that is, because of the behaviour of other states. There have been few conflicts between states since 1945 that have not involved third and fourth parties, and especially the great powers. Most major internal conflicts have also involved third parties: conflicts in India before partition, in Yemen before British withdrawal, in Cyprus before Britain and then Greece and Turkey accepted a Cypriot desire for independence, and in states under Soviet and United States influence. Conflict is itself engendered by the disunity and scapegoating that enters into local relationships when national aspirations are frustrated. It is exacerbated when one or more of the parties has an expectation of, or actual support from, an external power. While, therefore, parties to a dispute have an interest from the point of view of resolving conflict in altering the behaviour of other states and eliminating their influence, they are usually both powerless and unwilling to do this, at least until other states lose interest, and the costs of conflict are reassessed by one of the parties. There are, consequently, limitations imposed upon the freedom of parties in disputes to act, and therefore upon the subjective nature of their conflict. In this sense conflict frequently involves, especially at its early stages, objective and irreconcilable differences. Attention has been drawn to the need to analyse relationships at local levels of conflict, in simulated isolation from external influences. One purpose is to restore the subjective and manipulative element in the relationships of the local parties to help them see more clearly the costs and consequences of foreign support, and the ways in which it may prolong conflict without altering the final outcome.

(iii) MEANS OF COSTING

There is implied in this reasoning the existence of a high degree of rationality in decision-making. This is a sound hypothesis. Decisions may not appear to be rational to third parties; but governments respond to circumstances in ways that are calculated to maximise their advantages, and their decisions must be regarded as reasoned regardless of the consequences.

Less credible are other implied assumptions: first that means exist by which values can be placed in an order of preference, second that there is some way of costing values so that they can be compared with costs of achieving them, and third that costs of achieving a particular goal can be predicted with any degree of accuracy.

These difficulties are inherent in political decision-making. The political process is the allocation of values, and decisions about the sacrifice of resources that should be made to acquire and to preserve them. However, the claim is being made that conflict that is more costly than the values to be achieved can be avoided by theoretical analysis and controlled communication. This requires some support, having in mind the more traditional and apparently reasonable one that political decision-making is an art, and does not lend itself to accurate prediction and costing.

There are two issues here (both dealt with in the companion study). The first is the rationalisation by governments of costs incurred by adding new values whenever costs exceed expectations. A limited war to defend an innocent victim of aggression can readily become a war to defend all peoples against aggression, or a war to end war. This is a subjective process – sometimes almost an unconscious one – and can be analysed in such a way as to trace out the course of escalation in values and the reasons for it. Parties can be helped to see how current goals have developed out of original ones, and the ephemeral nature of some of these rationalised goals.

The second issue is the feasibility of prediction. A traditional and historically derived view is that political prediction is not possible except in the same sense that statistically it can be predicted that a certain number of car accidents will happen on a particular road over a given period of time. Each is a unique event which cannot be predicted. Governments must act in ways calculated to promote their interests, with all the means at their disposal, and cannot calculate the outcome of their decisions, just as a driver must perform as best he can, without knowing whether or not he will become a statistic. What the behavioural scientist tries to do is to find out more about behaviours that are and are not costly – the behaviours that increase and decrease road accidents. If independence and nationalism are found to be values strongly held, then any policy of a state that challenges these is likely to be costly to that state, and attempts to suppress movements of social and political reform in conditions in which peoples feel they are being denied felt needs are likely to fail or to be costly. If political adjustment is inhibited by expectations of foreign support, the amount of support required will be greater than appeared originally to be required. Deterrence, escalation, prejudice and misperception and all aspects of decision-making are the subject of behavioural propositions. By considering these, many of which are drawn from sources in addition to international politics, a better assessment of costs, and more reliable predictions might be possible. If consideration is given to general propositions in circumstances in which parties can test them in relation to their own conflict, and in the presence of each other, at least some of the hit and miss of political judgement should be eliminated. The proposition that meaningful prediction is not possible is unacceptable. The proposition that in our present state of knowledge prediction of political probabilities is not at a high level is unchallengeable. Controlled communication is a means of increasing the state of knowledge, and increasing the probabilities of accurate prediction.

(iv) THE ACTOR AS DECISION-MAKER

An assumption of controlled communication is that conformity brought about by external coercion, by the power of one party or by the intervention of third parties, cannot be stable. The individual unit in a behavioural system is integrated into it by identifying with its interests and values, and not as a result of coercion within it. Once again, if General Systems Theory is applied, this is axiomatic. A system responds and learns as an integrated whole. If required to conform to some pattern of behaviour determined and enforced by an outside agent, either the system will attempt to reject this coercion, or there will be internal system change, leading to internal conflict, and ultimately to aggression against the external coercive influence. Examples abound of frustrated independence of peoples, and there is empirical evidence of internal conflict followed by aggression against external states. India, Egypt, China and Algeria at various stages of their history are familiar cases.

A state is a responsible institution: it and it alone must take final responsibility for the protection of the values and interests of those who rely upon it. States enter into agreements, and any dispute arising out of these can be settled only by them: they cannot hand over treaty making or remaking to any foreign authority. If a state changes its policies or its values, treaties must change. This is not to say that a state is entirely free to make and undo relationships: continuity, consistency and reliability in behaviour are basic to its working relationships, and a state includes these relationships in its values. The rules that bind states are those that each finds it must observe to preserve the values it has, including peaceful relationships with other states. These are rules of decision-making, and foreign policy-making.

Legal idealists who have advocated judicial and enforced approaches to the settlement of conflict have been advocating the universal adoption of procedures that are in many cases not only unrealistic, but procedures that, if applied, would frequently tend to be destructive of stable states, and of peaceful international relations. The 'peace through law' approach is a logical one only on one assumption: that power or coercion is ultimately the controlling influence. If it is assumed that independence in the pursuit of state values is behaviourally unnecessary, and that the power of greater states in practice can dominate effectively the behaviour of smaller ones, then order through coercion and law is a logical objective, but not otherwise. By this it is not meant to imply that law has no role: the formulation of law is, like etiquette, an inducement for its observance. However, the law must reflect the sociological needs and interests of those expected to conform with it.

A corollary is that the resolution of conflict must come from the parties themselves: it is only they that can arrive at value judgements of the complicated kind required in the resolution of conflict. Any proposals that come from a mediator or another state are likely to be framed within a set of values and interests that are not those of the parties.

It also follows that cooperation between social groups is possible only on the basis of independence of units involved. In the contemporary world this is apparent. States are tending to break up into smaller ethnic or tribal units which were formed in the past often by foreign powers, and which have continued under the control of newly created governments. The probability is that functional cooperation, federations and integration rest finally upon the independent decision-making of the groups involved, and that before world society is charac- terised by increased integration it must go through a stage of increased disintegration or reaction against external controls of communities that seek independence in their decision-making. Scottish and French Canadian national- ism, tribal conflict in Nigeria and Turkish Cypriot insis- tence upon partition in Cyprus, were reactions against coercive influences upon communities that wished to determine their own values and interests.

(v) THE DISCOVERY OF SUB-GROUPS

The significance of developments towards more detailed studies by methods which take into account a greater number of real data is that phenomena of interest to political scientists, such as conflict, are found to consist of classes or sub-groups that require separate treatment. For example, in economics unemployment is no longer regarded as one single social phenomenon, as it was when it was thought to be due to laziness or lack of individual initiative. There is structural unemployment, transitional unemployment, unemployment created by financial policies, the unemployment of school-leavers. Each of these categories can be broken down into sub-groups. For example, school-leavers include some who know what they want to do and are searching for it, others who drift into any occupation, still others who need to be directed and helped to find suitable employment, and these categories are found to relate to social background and opportunity. The causes are different, and the means of overcoming the condition are different. So, too, in communal and inter-state conflict. Traditional legal approaches to conflicts regard the phenomenon as a single one, and normative rules are set down to deal with it. Consequently the implication is that all aggression is illegal or morally wrong, and that all defence against aggression is justified. This reflects the implied legal view that violence is evil and needs to be suppressed or resisted. But this is a superficial, though perhaps politically convenient way in which aggression and violence have been regarded in the past. In practice the threat of violence employed to maintain a structure may be no less destructive to society and its development than the use of violence to change a structure. This is the *status quo*–revisionist situation stated in another way. It points to the existence of different motivations of conflict and violence, and therefore different phenomena requiring different treatments. The violence associated with the period of discovery and expansion of states is quite different from the violence associated with struggles against colonialism and feudalism. The violence employed by the United States in Latin America is different in motivation from the violence used within the United States by Negroes. Almond and Powell argue: 'One obvious means of articulating demands is through physical demonstrations of violence. . . . For this reason it is important to distinguish between (a) spontaneous violence by anomic interest groups, and (b) violence and demonstrations as a means of access which any group may use. . .'.[4] It is all designated violence; but there are characteristic differences just as there are differences in forms of unemployment. International conflict differs from age to age, and takes different forms at any one time. It is the setting, the circumstances, which determine whether violence is a relevant response. It is all called conflict, or aggression; but giving it a common name does not make it the same phenomenon. Unless the condition that is to be controlled is precisely and accurately determined, the means of dealing with it are likely to be ineffective if not counterproductive. Diagnosis in medicine determines treatment. It has proved unproductive and even self-defeating to treat delinquents and some psychopaths as one would treat a car driver who has infringed some law of the road, or a businessman who knowingly and deliberately has attempted to avoid an agreement. Legal and normative approaches to social problems have tended not to differentiate between types of violence.

It needs to be made clear that in making these distinctions no ideologies or value judgements are involved. One is not saying that violence to upset the *status quo* is more or is less justifiable than violence to maintain it. There are analytical differences. One could take a functional view of conflict and argue that without conflict there cannot be social development. In the absence of effective means of peaceful change this is probably so. Nevertheless, action taken to prevent change, even though it is successful in the short term in preventing violence, is likely to lead to greater outbursts of violence such as occurred in two world wars. Conflicts may be more functional and less destructive when they are allowed to come to the surface as they occur, than when they are suppressed. This is especially so if means of peaceful change are available. The relevance of controlled communication is that it provides a cost-means of assessing interests, and therefore a means of peaceful change.

(vi) PERSONS AND STATES

There is an implied assumption here that changes which take place in the perceptions and values of individuals can be transferred to the nations or states which they represent. There are two separate processes involved, first transmission from representatives around the table to formal decision-makers, and second the transfer of altered perspectives from the formal decision-makers to their electorates.

The first process is the clear-cut one of reporting, and there are various devices that assist representatives in transmitting their altered attitudes and their increased information to their principals. This is a process which is inherent in diplomacy and representation at international conferences.

The second process raises problems of leadership and the use of mass media. However, it is not as complicated as might seem at first sight. The analysis of conflict by controlled communication leads to altered perceptions, and reassessment of values in relation to costs of conflict. But these are not ends in themselves. The purpose of the exercise is to discover alternatives, options not previously considered, and different means of attaining existing goals. While it might be impossible for leadership to alter attitudes and stereotypes within a community, it might not be impossible to promote different approaches to existing goals and even to advocate goals previously not considered. The Middle East and Vietnam problems in 1968 were problems of finding politically acceptable means of attaining stated goals, which would not seem to be a fundamental change in policy or the sacrifice of important political values. Some political device, such as a change of leadership as took place in Indonesia, an election on a particular platform as took place in Cyprus, (or a declaration by a president not to accept re-nomination as occurred in the United States) might be required to mark the beginning of a new direction. Controlled communication, because it sets out to help to discover possible new directions, does not necessarily require that the perception and value changes that take place among people around the table must also take place within the governments and communities in conflict.

(vii) TESTING OF HYPOTHESES

These are some of the main assumptions and hypotheses that are implied in the use of the technique of controlled communication. They contradict those that adapt conventional approaches to inter-nation and inter-state conflict and its control. It is assumptions and hypotheses about conflict and its control that most guide future state policies and the construction and operation of international institutions concerned with security. Coercive techniques, both legal and military, have failed to achieve their purposes; but their failure in itself does not give any reason for believing others are likely to succeed. How can these assumptions and hypotheses be tested?

If in many situations it were found that resolution of conflict by controlled communication were achieved, this would give some support to the validity and reliability of the technique, and for the implied assumptions about the nature of world society. However, in a research project no such reality testing is possible. If the Secretary-General of the United Nations were to provide that all mediators appointed by him should adopt this technique in the next ten cases, and if it were adopted in some test cases, as for example, in relation to the stalemate of North–South Korea, then some findings would be possible, not only about the technique, but more importantly about the nature of conflict and of world society. In the absence of such reality testing, other means must be found.

The relevant question in this report is to what extent, if any, can there be conclusions from a limited number of experiences of controlled communication, from related discussions with members of governments and from their representatives, and from the field work and involvement in other situations with which it is associated?

Clearly it is not possible to generalise from a few cases when the cases themselves are the only source of data. For example, public opinion surveys need to be based upon an adequate sample when there is complete reliance upon the survey as a source of information from which to estimate the state of public opinion. It follows that nothing in the way of testing or conclusions can be drawn from a limited number of experiences of controlled communication – whatever might be their value in stimulating hypotheses. All that can be said is that communication was established where previously it did not exist, perception and attitudes of participants altered during the exercise, and events followed, some of which could have been directly or indirectly related, but which could have been due no less to many other influences that were operating on the parties simultaneously.

When, however, the source of data is outside the immediate area of investigation, when, that is, there are extrapolations and deductive reasoning, there can be generalisations from very few cases. If by extrapolation from other surveys or tests in other fields it were hypothesised that the higher the level of unemployment the greater would be opposition to the government in power, and if other tested propositions of this kind were advanced to take account of a large number of variables, the opinion surveys would not be primarily a source of data, but the means by which the validity of the propositions was tested. Starting with a presumption of a high probability, a few cases should indicate the validity of a proposition. Even one case could be sufficient in some circumstances: the one testing of an atomic bomb is sufficient to demonstrate the validity of theories and techniques involved.

Probability can be established in many ways according to the circumstances. Drugs are tested first on animals, thus establishing a probability of reaction on humans before being tried on them. A few tests are sufficient when the drug is designed to affect a local muscle, far more when the brain is affected. In other words, both the deductive reasoning that is available and the complexity of the conditions being affected are relevant in considering the number of tests required. In the field of our present interest both the amount of analogous reasoning and the complexity of the conditions being examined vary greatly. The testing of the proposition that a mediator will be less acceptable the more he goes to and fro between parties presenting their viewpoints, presents few problems. The proposition that coercion is self-defeating and self-adjusting processes are effective as means of resolving conflict is more complex. A very large number of tests would be required because of the complexity of the conditions, unless adequate testing had been carried out on a large number of closely related circumstances.

The tendency in any one discipline must be for extrapolation and deductive reasoning to become more fruitful as a source of hypotheses as science progresses, that is, as observations and tested propositions in other and related fields of study accumulate. In the study of International Relations a recent reaction to a passing era of unsubstantiated generalisation has been a tendency for more and more statistical analysis. Greater precision is widely welcomed, but when operational definitions are determined by data available, statistical analysis is not always a wholly reliable substitute for reasoning from tested propositions in related behaviour, or for field work designed to obtain data of more direct relevance. The problem of extrapolation in international relations is dealt with by Kelman,[5] and it is one to which increasing attention must be given as interdisciplinary studies progress.

(viii) ANALOGOUS REASONING

The probability that controlled communication would produce predicted results was high because of experience in other behavioural fields. There has been a persistent movement, both in theoretical work and in social practice, away from coercion, punishment and threat as a means of controlling behaviour, and away from enforced settlements as a means of settling conflicts. The trend has been towards the treatment of antisocial behaviour at its source, towards attempts to resolve conflict by non-authoritative means, and towards a greater tolerance of non-conventional behaviour which previously might have been regarded as anti-social and controlled by coercion. Academically, and more and more frequently in practice, the irrelevance of punishment and deterrence has come to be recognised, both on grounds of their lack of effectiveness, and of their inability to produce the conditions that would eliminate anti-social behaviour. The trend appears to have been persistent for more than a century in Western countries.

It is in the field of education that there has been most comparative work done on conformity by coercion and by self-induced processes. While work done seems not to have been brought together in any one study, references are scattered throughout the literature of the last few decades.[6] Anderson found that there were marked differences in the behaviour of children under different teachers. Where the teachers used less domination and more integration the children were more attentive and cooperative, they were less restless, contributed more to the lesson, and showed greater spontaneity and initiative. Inevitably the question arose as to who initiated behaviour, the teacher or the children, since it might be argued that the behaviour of the teacher was adapted to meet the situations arising from the behaviour of the children. Further tests were conducted with control groups. 'There was little room for doubt that the behaviour of the children was a response to that of their teachers, and not vice versa.'[7] Lippett and White experimented with groups of boys imposing upon them three different types of control – autocratic, democratic and laissez faire. Autocracy provoked one of two reactions, submission or aggression amounting to open rebellion. Group morale, in the sense of spontaneous cohesion, was highest under democratic conditions and lowest under autocratic conditions. The laissez faire control led to dissatisfaction with levels of efficiency and to the vicious circle of frustration–aggression–frustration. A tendency to give way to a leader was noticed in these last circumstances.[8]

Perhaps the most sudden change from coercion to controlled self-adjustment has been in the field of social conformity and nonconformity, including anti-social behaviour and delinquency. It has been brought to attention by the activities of caseworkers, social and medical, who have been invited by courts after experience that punishment is no remedy. There have always been non-judicial means of dealing with delinquency. For example, the British Industrial Schools Act of 1966 was for this purpose. What is new is the work of the caseworker, of the medical profession, and of the teacher, all of whom seek to help the adjustment of the individual to society by supportive and not punitive methods, and also recognise some of the environmental preconditions of social nonconformity. One need only quote the concluding remarks of Boss:

> This book began with a statement to the effect that within little more than a century, social policy has been radically altered as the result of a profound change in attitude toward juvenile delinquency on the part of society. At one time the young offender was held morally as well as legally responsible for the crime he committed and in consequence, was expected to take his punishment however harsh it might be. In the course of time, ideas about moral culpability, legal responsibility and liability to punishment have undergone changes and these are reflected particularly in social policy. Some

people would consider the changes to have been for the worse, as yet another manifestation of a nation that is failing in its inculcation of moral values and a sense of personal responsibility into the younger generation. Others, however, would view them as a natural and logical extension in the social development of a society which, while it feels concern to the point of taking certain actions, is certainly not frightened by the delinquencies committed by its younger members, and is therefore prepared to deal with them on essentially educational and social welfare, rather than predominantly legal, lines.[9]

Reflecting upon the science of science, it can be argued that wars will be found to be no more due to state aggressiveness than delinquency is due to individual attributes. In both cases there is an interaction process between the subject and his environment. While environmental changes are sometimes possible and necessary, both the individual and the state need the insights that allow them to adjust to them. It can also be argued that it will be found that the way to avoid conflict, or to resolve it once it has occurred, will not be by the decisions of powerful states or some international institution with judicial and enforcement powers, but by processes that facilitate this adjustment of state to environment. Not unexpectedly, the practice of international politics is little more advanced than social practice in municipal society. The operative assumption in foreign policy-making is that the behaviour of states is anti-social in respect of world society. That state behaviour might not be deliberately anti-social, and merely a normal response to existing conditions within the range of existing knowledge, is commonly regarded as an idealistic and unreal view – as were earlier claims about the nature of the unemployed and of delinquents.

Behavioural thinking has also been moving away from

the belief that social interaction must involve conflict because of the struggle for scarce resources and positions. In most cases of social interaction, for example industrial conflict, the gain of one side does not equal the loss of the other; there are behavioural variables that render interaction far more complicated than this. Solutions are possible that enable both sides to gain, as for example, when conditions of industrial peace lead to increased productivity. Modern management is becoming aware of this, and far more attention is being given than in any previous age to forms of participation by employees that once would have been thought to amount to a loss to management, but which in modern conditions are claimed to be a gain.

Taken together, these trends away from coercion, and away from treating conflict as zero sum, are determining the trends within behavioural studies. If we were to draw two axes, the x axis representing coercion at the negative extreme and cooperation and participation of the subject at the positive end, and the y axis representing, at the negative extreme, solutions to conflicts where the gain of one side equals the loss of the other, and gains to both sides at the positive end, then we would have four quadrants that depict approaches to social problems. On the bottom left would be compulsory settlements of disputes where there were apparently irreconcilable conflicts of interests: this was how social problems were once regarded and tackled. On the top left would be conditions in which even conflicts that could be settled to the advantage of all parties had to be determined by an outside agent and enforced. On the bottom right would be conditions in which no solutions were possible because there were conditions of irreconcilable conflicts of interests, and no authority to impose settlements. This is a condition of anarchy, and many describe international relations in these terms. On the top right there would be a condition in which conflicts had a solution that would satisfy all parties, and which would therefore be maintained without enforcement.

Positive sum: ↑	both sides can gain from the resolution of the conflict.
Compulsory Settlement Procedures:	Contemporary Resolution Procedures:
based on belief that behaviour is the result of 'evil' intent or of 'self interest', hence the need for deterrence or punishment.	based on belief that behaviour is a reaction to the environment.
Zero-sum: ↓	the gain of one side equals the loss of the other.

It is in this last segment that controlled communication would fit. However, instead of assuming that states could solve problems peacefully, face-to-face techniques postulate that there are misperceptions of relationships and inadequate information about alternative means and alternative goals, and that institutionalised means are required to enable states to reperceive and to obtain information about the motivations and goals of each other. The underlying assumption is that states are not in themselves a cause of conflict, aggressive, or power motivated, but that they are responding to their environment within the limits of the knowledge they have available about their interests and the responses of others. Given perfect knowledge of responses of others, or tested theories and rules of conduct that could act as a substitute for perfect foresight, states would avoid any conflicts that were more costly than alternative means of achieving their goals. This proposition is argued at length in the complementary study that arose out of face-to-face discussions.

It is the sociology of conflict, and the handling of disputes within a state but outside judicial processes, that can throw light upon international conflict and international relations generally; it is the solving of the conflict problem, rather than the determination and enforcement of a settlement, that is what is sought both in these social conflicts and in international relations. Furthermore, while the study of small group conflict is relevant to international conflict in that neither can be resolved by judicial and enforcement processes, there is frequently a causal connection between internal conflicts and international conflict, as for example, when communal conflicts spill over into international relations.

(ix) CONCLUSIONS

We are in this study dealing with two different academic subjects, and behaviour at two different levels. One is what appears empirically to be the nature of state and system behaviour, and the other is what state and system behaviour is likely to be in conditions in which a third party is present to demonstrate the problems of perception and communication, or in conditions in which states and systems are managed in a context of conventional wisdom that includes an awareness of all the problems of decision-making. There are the 'what is' and a 'what would be' aspects, and there cannot be a clear separation. Indeed, even examining 'what is' tends to create 'what would be'. Abercrombie found that demonstrating how students perceive made them introspective and led to more accurate perception.[10] In controlled communication, the processes of examining the perceptions that parties in conflict have of each other alters their perceptions. This alteration of the condition being examined by reason of its examination is almost new to international studies because field work is relatively new. Sometimes the reader may obtain the impression that this research study is normatively or idealistically oriented because the changes that occur are presumably productive of improved relations; but this is incidental to the analysis. There is no theoretical reason why situations could not be designed to test hypotheses by increasing tensions deliberately – suspicions and misperceptions could be induced. What is being studied are the consequences of learning by the parties themselves. Niemeyer observed: 'What we have to do is to wait and be quiet; to stop our feverish efforts to do something. The next word is not with *us*, but with reality'.[11] What he was implying was that international coercive systems could not be imposed on states; we have to await developments within states. The developments for which we must wait are learning ones. If these can be induced, not only generally by increasing universal conventional wisdom, but specifically in respect of particular situations, then the avoidance and resolution of conflict might be promoted.

The sources of data and hypotheses in the study of the complex phenomenon of international conflict are diplomatic history, general pre-theorising and extrapolations suggested by experience and experiment in other behavioural disciplines, the empirical and statistical data available as a result of national statistics and private research, contrived situations such as simulations, and specific work which a particular project seems to require in the absence of available data. All have a role to play. Some processes may be more fruitful than others. The diplomatic historian has limited data already selected in accordance with the notions of the period, and on the quantitative side, the analyst of existing data is confined by it, and in any event is likely to be harbouring the traditional notions of the diplomatic historian. The theoriser and extrapolator may be able to suggest hypotheses of greater relevance and interest, and those interested in contrived situations and field work may be able to supply data not otherwise available.

In this project there has been a useful combination of approaches. The preparation for controlled communication involved, in the first place, an examination of available theoretical literature, not only in the area of world politics, but in the behavioural studies relevant to conflict. Comparative studies of conflict situations in the contemporary period are relevant, even when they are written up only at the superficial level on which such situations are usually reported. Typologies of conflict are attempted as part of the research project. By these means it is possible to prepare in advance what appear to be relevant questions and propositions. The controlled communication itself corrects prior assumptions, directs attention to questions not previously posed, and leads to a re-examination of available theories and data, in addition to suggesting additional field work that is required. The field work supplies data, suggests other perspectives and propositions that feed back into theorising and the formulation of further questions. Pre-theorising or deductive reasoning from similar work in other disciplines remains the most important indication of probability of the validity of propositions before controlled communication takes place.

NOTES TO CHAPTER TWELVE

(1) See companion study, ch. 1.
(2) Dienes and Jeeves, *Thinking in Structures*, pp. 115 ff.

(3) Sir Fred Bartlett, quoted in Dienes, *Mathematics in Primary Education*, p. 19.

(4) Almond and Powell, *Comparative Politics*, p. 81.

(5) Kelman (ed.), *International Behavior*.

(6) See, for example, Gardner, *Experiment and Tradition in Primary Schools*; Wall, *Education and Mental Health*; Wills, *Throw Away Thy Rod*; Batten, *The Non-Directive Approach*.

(7) See Evans, *Sociometry and Education*, p. 103.

(8) The Lippett and White experiment is reported by them in a contribution 'The Social Climate of Children's Groups' in Barker *et al*, *Child Behavior and Development*.

(9) Boss, *Social Policy and the Young Delinquent*, p. 94.

(10) See Abercrombie, *The Anatomy of Judgement*.

(11) Niemeyer, *Law Without Force*.

13 Assessment

The bringing of parties to an on-going communal or inter-state dispute into a situation of controlled communication is an obvious way of examining their relations, of stimulating theories, of arriving at hypotheses and of testing them. One might wonder why it has not been done before.

(i) THE SCIENCE OF SCIENCE

Looking back on the history of any area of study one is struck by two separate, and apparently conflicting, features. The first is the simplicity and obviousness of the most recent discovery, and more particularly, of solutions to problems. Gravity, the roundness of the earth, mass and velocity as components of momentum, trace elements in soils, hovercraft, kitchen gadgets, and all manner of physical and chemical phenomena that were once beyond the comprehension of thinkers are now part of everyday life, and apparently generally understood by very great numbers of peoples. The mysteries of flying, nuclear science, plumbing, carpentry, medicine, computers and pig raising vanish with training and knowledge that is readily acquired by more and more people. It is the experience of many of us that years and years of writing and re-thinking about a seemingly complex problem lead to propositions and forms of exposition so obvious that communication of them by publication seems unnecessary; yet we are aware that we moved a long way from our starting point. Especially is this so in the social sciences. Contemporary textbooks on the philosophy of education are merely stating what seems, once stated, to be common sense. When once explained, what could be more obvious than the expansion of credit in times of recession, the treatment of delinquency by remedial and non-judicial means, or the need for cleanliness to ensure health? Teachers of university students soon find that they bore their students with criticisms of outmoded theories: students are more attracted by the thinking of 'frontiersmen' than that of traditionalists, and absorb it more quickly, because it seems to them more credible. The greater the insights into a problem, the easier is understanding, even though the greater are the number of variables, and the more elaborate are the techniques. There is thus a simplicity in science, despite its apparent procedural complexities, which is absent in the elusive concepts of metaphysics and unsubstantiated generalisation.

This consideration gives rise to a second one. The history of thought in any one subject reveals tortuous steps, the mere glimmerings of solutions for years before they are found, and tentative hypotheses that in retrospect seem to have been absurd, or contrary to phenomena then observable. Yet the thinker of the past was as aware and as intelligent as the present day one. The conclusion must be that history of thought in any one area of study is incomplete without the social, political, economic, philosophical and other environments in which it took place. How, otherwise, could laziness have been mistaken for structural unemployment at the beginning of the industrial revolution, wealth and power for social rights, or inabilities to adjust to social demands for lack of 'breeding' at a time when there were educational opportunities only for the few? Thought in any one area is conditioned by the total environment. There is continuity, and in this sense every idea can be traced back and back giving rise to an assertion that there is nothing new in thought; but the patterns of thought in any area are constantly changing due to discovery, innovation and invention in the total environment. Behaviour perceived as lazy in one set of conditions or state of knowledge might be perceived as ill-health or the result of economic conditions in another. Sickness or death perceived as the result of punishment by the gods in one state of knowledge is perceived in another as being due to disease. The cumulative effects of science operate through the total environment – each new pattern of thought affects others.

It is the linguistic environment that best reflects the total environment of the thinker, for it is language that relates areas of thought. Social theory has its parallel in inventive achievement: the analogies used to explain behaviour have been drawn from the physical environment and the successive discoveries of society. The language of the day draws the boundaries of possible thought in that day: language is a tool of thought as well as of communication, and each new model, each added 'jargon' borrowed from another area of thought, extends these boundaries. The rate of discovery in any one field affects the rate in others.

It follows that new areas of thought, that is areas relating to the most recent social experiences, of which international politics is one, do not start from scratch and work through the developments that have already occurred in the study of other fields of behaviour. If, after hundreds of years of thinking, it is found that the behaviour of a subject is determined by a reaction between it and its environment, then this is a starting point for any new area of thought involving a subject and an environment. If there are found to be certain social interactions that are better regulated by controlled face-to-face discussion than by, for example, judicial processes, then this is a starting point. Happily international relations as a discipline has a take-off point many hundreds of years ahead of the take-off point of social studies generally. What appears to be an obvious method now appears this way because of the environment provided by other sciences. Face-to-face techniques are now applied to communal and international conflict because of the techniques developed in the last decade or so in psychology, delinquency and psychiatry, and because of models advanced in cybernetics, economics, electronics and many other studies.

(ii) THE LIMITATIONS AND ADVANTAGES OF THE METHOD

Controlled communication as applied to international politics has problems of greater magnitude than usually arise. There are not the many thousands of cases with which the social caseworker deals. Moreover, each study is an expensive and time-consuming business, and the number of studies made is likely to be relatively small. There are also special problems relating to recording data once generated. Discussion between persons whose governments are in conflict is necessarily approached with caution by them; it would destroy the informal and off-the-record nature of the discourse to introduce tape recorders, video tapes, or other devices which would make possible a detailed analysis of responses, of alteration in perceptions, of the cause of these, of the influence of the personalities of parties and panel members, of changes in moods, and of other data of value. It is particularly important to have these data when considering techniques of conflict resolution, and it is important also for an understanding of the nature of conflict, and of international relations generally. The notes and observations of panel members must remain the only source of data generated at the time of discussion.

In addition, there are special problems arising out of the fact that individuals, no matter how high they are in the decision-making apparatus, cannot reflect the points of view and attitudes of their states, at least unless the discussions are so arranged as to permit frequent consultation with cabinet ministers and others concerned. Even so there are difficulties. Persons around the table are likely to reperceive the nature of the conflict once its origins are analysed, and once the motivations and attitudes of the antagonists become clear. In cases in which the conflict has existed for a long time, popular attitudes are firmly established. The altered perception of the person around the table cannot always be conveyed to others who have not had the experience of the discussions. In these circumstances the exercise may have to be performed again in ways which involve the final decision-makers. It is in this respect that there is a significant difference between this form of casework and that of the social caseworker who is dealing directly with individuals, or small groups, involved in a conflict.

The technique has some obvious limitations from a research point of view. It imposes severe restraints upon scholars participating. Parties engaged in violent conflicts cannot be expected to respond to a request to meet, even for academic purposes, unless not only what transpires, but even the fact of meeting is secret. The position is even more delicate than the professional–client relationship in law or medicine, where it is possible to refer to cases without identification of persons. The secrecy aspect inhibits discussion among colleagues, injects into academic life an unwelcome element, and imposes some restraints upon the publication of research papers. However, this is no new experience; it is becoming more and more familiar as interaction between government and scholar develops. There are means of generalisation after many separate analyses.

Subject to these limitations, this method applied to international studies shares the advantages of similar methods applied in other fields. First, the whole of a particular situation is examined – economic, political, constitutional, social, strategic, cultural, religious and all other aspects. Second, if the original hypotheses are shown to be inadequate, the same situation or another can be re-examined by this method. The situation being analysed is not an abstraction, as are simulated and historically recorded ones; all the data required to examine any set of hypotheses are available.

(iii) THE INSTITUTIONALISATION OF CONFLICT RESOLUTION

The White House Conference on International Cooperation of 1965, and in particular the Committee on Peaceful Settlement of Disputes, strongly urged further enquiry into conciliation, and 'that continuing emphasis and study be given to the procedures and conceptual framework of conflict resolution by peaceful means, drawing on the data of historical research, considering the potentialities of the United Nations and the approaches of the social sciences, with a view to providing insights and perspectives to parties involved in international disputes'.[1]

The institutional approach to peaceful settlement has been discredited by failure. Theoretical and analytical approaches have preoccupied scholars where previously they were concerned with the potentialities of the League and the United Nations. But this has not been a rejection of international institutions as such. On the contrary, functionalism has become an integral part of theoretical thinking. It was a particular type of international institution that was being rejected. Behavioural theories are now leading back into institutional applications that take into account the altered nature of world society, and the insights now available into behavioural responses.

What we all finally seek is the institutionalisation of conflict resolution, by one process or another. If judicial procedures are not effective in many cases then others need to be found. In industrial and social life, the non-judicial resolution of conflict has been functionalised; industrial courts of enquiry, business firms that undertake enquiries into industrial conflicts, family guidance councils, are examples. The techniques are still primitive, but experience is leading to new insights into the nature of conflict, and to improved techniques. The research worker and the practitioner are often the one person. There seems to be no reason why procedures on conflict resolution should not be systematised and institutionalised in international relations as in social relations, especially if they can be devised so as not to involve political decisions at least until the basis of resolution is suggested by the process. International functionalism has developed in many areas in which states find they need to cooperate; they are at present confined to the economic and non-political areas. Functional organisation for the resolution of conflict is the logical bridge between traditional functionalism, and that area of power politics which has so far been resistant to treatment. Stated in another way, the rule of law is a Western concept, and falls short of the needs and interests of international society at its present stage; the rule of consensus is an Eastern concept and is open to the influence of ideological and emotional excesses; the rule of sociological analysis avoids the static features of the one and the transitory features of the other.

Peacekeeping is beginning to be institutionalised, and procedures are being recorded. Mediation in serious international disputes is still by *ad hoc* decisions of the United Nations and the Secretary-General, and usually the direct application of traditional diplomatic skills. Are the diplomatic and legal professions the appropriate ones from which to select mediators, and is the United Nations framework a suitable one?

The tentative conclusions arrived at as a result of this study are, first, that conflict resolution is a specialised technique for which special training and experience are required. It is a technique that no one person can perform because the knowledge and experience required are beyond the capacity of any one person: a team is required. Second, a conflict resolution team needs to be free of directives and limitations, and could not operate effectively under a Security Council resolution, or be obligated to make reports on matters that are better not reported except in so far as the parties might desire themselves jointly to report. For this reason the institutional organisation required is probably that of an independent commission which can go into action without delay at the request of the parties concerned, call upon what technical assistance it requires, and operate freely to accomplish or to fail in its defined purposes. These conclusions are not incompatible with the main observation made in the companion study that increased professional knowledge within relevant departments of government is the main safeguard against conflict.

NOTE TO CHAPTER THIRTEEN

(1) The White House Conference on International Cooperation, National Citizens' Commission.

Bibliography

ABERCROMBIE, M. L. J. *The Anatomy of Judgement*. Hutchinson: London 1960.

ALBINSKI, H. S. *Australian Policies and Attitudes towards China*. Princeton UP 1965.

ALGER, C. F. 'Interaction in a Committee of the United Nations General Assembly', in *Quantitative International Politics: Insights and Evidence*, ed. J. D. Singer. Free Press: Chicago 1968.

ALMOND, G. A. and G. B. POWELL, *Comparative Politics*. Little, Brown: Boston 1966.

ATWATER, E., K. FORSTER and J. S. PRYBYLA, *World Tensions: Conflict and Accommodation*. Appleton-Century-Crofts: New York 1967.

BATTEN, T. R. *The Non-Directive Approach in Group and Community Work*. Oxford UP 1967.

BOSS, P. *Social Policy and the Young Delinquent*. Routledge & Kegan Paul: London 1967.

BRIERLY, J. L. *The Law of Nations*, 6th ed. Oxford UP 1963.

BROWN, M. 'A Review of Casework Methods', in *New Developments in Casework*, ed. E. Younghusband. Allen & Unwin: London 1966.

BURTON, J. W. *Systems, States, Diplomacy and Rules*. Cambridge UP 1968.

BURTON, J. W. 'Western Intervention in South East Asia', *Year Book of World Affairs*, eds Keeton & Schwarzenberger, vol. 20. Stevens: London 1966.

BURTON, J. W. *Peace Theory*. Knopf: New York 1962.

CAMPBELL, D. T. 'Ethnocentric and Other Altruistic Motives', in *The Nebraska Symposium on Motivation 1965*, ed. D. Levine. Nebraska Press 1965.

CLARK, G. and L. B. SOHN. *World Peace Through World Law.* Harvard UP 1960.

CLAUDE, I. L. *Swords into Plowshares,* 2nd ed. Random House: 1963.

COSER, L. A. *The Functions of Social Conflict.* Routledge & Kegan Paul: London 1956.

COSER, L. A. *Continuities in the Study of Social Conflict.* Free Press: New York 1967.

David Davies Memorial Institute of International Studies. *Report of a Study Group on the Peaceful Settlement of International Disputes.* London 1966.

DENTON, F. H. 'Some Regularities in International Conflict, 1820–1949', in *Background,* vol. 9, no. 4.

DEUTSCH, K. W. *Nerves of Government.* Free Press: New York 1963.

DIENES, Z. P. and M. A. JEEVES. *Thinking in Structures.* Hutchinson: London 1965.

DIENES, Z. P. *Mathematics in Primary Education.* UNESCO Institute of Education: Hamburg 1965.

EVANS, K. M. *Sociometry and Education.* Routledge & Kegan Paul: London 1962.

FOSS, B. M. *New Horizons in Psychology.* Penguin Books: Harmondsworth 1966.

FOX, W. T. R. (ed), *Theoretical Aspects of International Relations.* Columbia UP 1959.

FRIEDMANN, W. *The Changing Structure of International Law.* Stevens: London 1964.

GARDNER, D. E. M. *Experiment and Tradition in Primary Schools.* Methuen: London 1966.

GUETZKOW, H. (ed), *Simulation in International Relations.* Prentice-Hall: Englewood Cliffs 1963.

HAAS, E. B. *Beyond the Nation-State.* Stanford UP 1964.

HANDY, R., and P. KURTZ, *A Current Appraisal of the Behavioral Sciences.* Behavioral Research Council: Washington D.C. 1964.

HARRISON, H. V. (ed), *The Role of Theory in International Relations.* Van Nostrand: Princeton 1964.

HIGGINS, R. *Conflict of Interests.* Bodley Head: London 1965.

HIGGINS, R. 'Policy Considerations and the International Judicial Process', in *International and Comparative Law Quarterly,* vol. 17, no. 1.

IKLE, F. C. *How Nations Negotiate.* Harper & Row: New York 1964.

JANDA, K. *Data Processing.* Northwestern UP 1965.

JENKS, C. W. *Law in the World Community*. Longmans: London 1967.

JERVIS, R. 'Hypotheses of Misperception', in *World Politics*, vol. XX, no. 3.

KAHN, H., and A. J. WIENER, *The Year 2000*. Collier-Macmillan: New York 1967.

KELMAN, H. C. (ed), *International Behavior*. Holt, Rinehart & Winston: New York 1965.

KERLINGER, F. N. *Foundations of Behavioral Research*. Holt, Rinehart & Winston: New York 1966.

LALL, A. *Modern International Negotiation*. Columbia UP: New York 1966.

LEWIN, L. C. (ed), *Report from Iron Mountain on the Possibility and Desirability of Peace*. Macdonald: London 1967.

LIPPETT, R. O. and R. K. WHITE, 'The Social Climate of Children's Groups', in R. G. Barker *et al.*, *Child Behavior and Development*. McGraw-Hill: New York 1943.

LUARD, E. *Conflict and Peace in the Modern International System*. Little, Brown: Boston 1968.

MACIVER, R. M. *Social Causation*. Ginn: London 1942.

MEEHAN, E. J. *The Theory and Method of Political Analysis*. The Dorsey Press: London 1965.

MEYER, A. S. 'Functions of the Mediator in Collective Bargaining', *Industrial and Labor Relations Review*, vol. 13. no. 2.

MITRANY, D. *A Working Peace System*. Oxford UP 1946.

MODELSKI, G. 'The International Relations of Internal War', in *International Aspects of Civil Strife*. ed. J. Rosenau. Princeton UP 1964.

NIEMEYER, G. *Law Without Force*. Princeton UP 1941.

NORTH, R. C., O. R. HOLSTI, M. G. ZANINOVICH, D. A. ZIENES, *Content Analysis: A Handbook with Applications for the Study of International Cases*. Northwestern UP: Evanston U.S.A. 1963.

POPPER, K. R. *The Poverty of Historicism*, Routledge & Kegan Paul: London 1957.

RUSSETT, B. M. *International Regions and the International System*. Rand McNally: Chicago 1967.

SCHWARZENBERGER, G. *Power Politics*, 3rd ed. Stevens: London 1964.

SHAMUYARIRA, N. *Crisis in Rhodesia*. Deutsch: London 1965.

SINGER, J. D. 'Data-making in International Relations', in *Behavioral Science*, vol. 10, no. 1.

SKINNER, B. F. *Science and Human Behaviour*. Collier-Macmillan: New York 1953.

SNYDER, R. C. 'Some Perspectives on the Use of Experimental Techniques in the Study of International Relations', in *Simulation in International Relations*, ed. H. Guetzkow. Prentice-Hall: Englewood Cliffs 1963.

STONE, J. *Law and Policy in the Quest for Survival*. Australian Broadcasting Commission lecture series: Sydney 1960.

SUCI, G. J., P. H. TANNENBAUM, *The Measurement of Meaning*. Illinois UP 1957.

THYNE, J. M. *The Psychology of Learning and Techniques of Teaching*. University of London Press 1963.

United Nations Security Council documents S/6253 of 26 March 1965.

WALL, W. D. *Education and Mental Health*. UNESCO 1955.

WALTZ, K. N. *Man, the State and War*. Columbia UP: New York 1959.

White House Conference on International Cooperation, National Citizens' Commission, 28 Nov–1 Dec 1965.

WILLS, W. D. *Throw Away Thy Rod*. Gollancz, 1960.

YALEM, R. *Regionalism and World Order*. Public Affairs Press: Washington 1965.

YOUNG, O. R. *The Intermediaries*. Princeton UP 1967.

YOUNGHUSBAND, E. *New Developments in Casework*. Allen & Unwin: London 1966.

Index